THE VICTORY OF FAITH

New Testament
Sermons For
Lent And Easter

Mark J. Molldrem

CSS Publishing Company, Inc., Lima, Ohio

THE VICTORY OF FAITH

Copyright © 1997 by
CSS Publishing Company, Inc.
Lima, Ohio

All rights reserved. No part of this publication may be reproduced in any manner whatsoever without the prior permission of the publisher, except in the case of brief quotations embodied in critical articles and reviews. Inquiries should be addressed to: Permissions, CSS Publishing Company, Inc., P.O. Box 4503, Lima, Ohio 45802-4503.

Scripture quotations are from the *New Revised Standard Version of the Bible*, copyright 1989 by the Division of Christian Education of the National Council of the Churches of Christ in the USA. Used by permission.

The Magnificat: Luther's Commentary, copyright © 1956, Concordia Publishing House. Used with permission.

Library of Congress Cataloging-in-Publication Data

Molldrem, Mark J.
    The victory of faith : sermons for Lent and Easter / Mark J. Molldrem.
      p. cm.
    ISBN 0-7880-1005-0 (pbk.)
    1. Lenten sermons. 2. Holy-Week sermons. 3. Easter—Sermons. 4. Sermons, American. I. Title.
BV4277.M64   1997
252'.6—dc21   96-37185
                                                                                    CIP

The book is available in the following formats, listed by ISBN:
    0-7880-1005-0   Book

PRINTED IN U.S.A.

*Dedicated to the memory of
Rev. Oscar C. Hanson*

Table Of Contents

Preface	7
Foreword	9
The Righteousness Of God 2 Corinthians 5:20b—6:10 Ash Wednesday	11
Adoption Into God's Family 1 Peter 3:18-22 Lent 1	17
The Gospel Of Our Calling Romans 4:13-25 Lent 2	21
The Word Of The Cross Is The Power Of God 1 Corinthians 1:18-25 Lent 3	27
As Is Ephesians 2:1-10 Lent 4	31
Prayer Clothes Hebrews 5:5-10 Lent 5	35
Obedience Philippians 2:5-11 Passion/Palm Sunday	41

Friday — The Good One   45
    Hebrews 10:16-25
    Good Friday

Witnesses   49
    1 Corinthians 15:1-11
    Easter Day

Made — Lost — And Found   53
    1 John 1:1—2:2
    Easter 2

New Life From Old   57
    1 John 3:1-7
    Easter 3

Love In Action   63
    1 John 3:16-24
    Easter 4

Love And Friendship   67
    1 John 4:7-21
    Easter 5

The Victory Of Faith   73
    1 John 5:1-6
    Easter 6

The Name Of Names   79
    Ephesians 1:15-23
    Ascension Day

Life In His Name   83
    1 John 5:9-13
    Easter 7

Preface

On Wednesday evening October 21, 1963, while a junior in high school, I received the Call into the ministry of the church. Pastor Oscar C. Hanson, a dear friend of our family, was preaching a series of sermons at Pontoppidan Lutheran Church in Fargo, North Dakota, which happened to be the church where my parents were married. It was a "preaching, teaching, reaching" kind of program for the congregation and he was the guest presenter. I had gone to his Sunday evening service already. Since this was the last evening of the series, I did not want to miss it and decided to go. There was a big football game against our archrivals that night, but I figured I could catch the second half. I caught more than I figured.

Or perhaps it would be better to say that I was caught. Up to this point in time, I had my sights pretty well set on becoming a high school biology teacher and basketball coach. These were two loves of mine at which I did very well and through which I experienced much joy. All that changed under a moon-bright autumn sky.

During the closing moments of Pastor Hanson's sermon, I had the strangest sensation. My whole being, that is to say my whole body and soul, filled with the shiver of another's presence. I felt transported beyond the sanctuary, while at the same time I was definitely in the sanctuary. I perceived a simple message directed to me: SERVE ME IN MY CHURCH. I did not hear this message; I did not see this message. I perceived it. I knew in an instant that this was my Call into the ministry. From that moment on, my life has been a straight trajectory through the seminary into the pulpit and the parish life of God's people.

This is the experience that has led me to dedicate this book to the memory and ministry of Oscar C. Hanson, whose preaching occasioned my Call into the ministry.

Preachers are not born. They are raised. I owe a great debt of gratitude to those who have raised me as a preacher of the gospel. There are more people than I can remember. But, I wish to acknowledge the following people of whom I am most conscious as having influenced my preaching: my father, Rev. Ariel Robert Molldrem, whom I have heard preach more than any other person; my grandfather, who admonished his grandson, "Preach Christ crucified, and only Christ"; Dr. Nelson Trout, who made sermons sing in my teenage ears; Dr. John C. Bates, whose eloquence gave me a sensual appreciation for language; Pastor Tande, who taught me that the content, not the style of a sermon, is by far the most important; Dr. Roy Harrisville, whose spirited, pithy sermons I would never miss while at seminary; Dr. Gerhard Forde, whose discernment of the Law and the Gospel has seared my soul; Shirley Jean Bennett Molldrem, my wife, who keeps me pastoral and down-to-earth; and my parishioners, without whose encouragement and examples of faith I would have given up long ago.

It should go without saying, yet it is important to say, that I owe my greatest debt to my Lord and Savior, Jesus Christ, who has called me into the ministry of Word and Sacrament. He has given me the purpose for my life, the message of truth to share, and the promise that it is not in vain.

What more could I want, then, than perhaps to be published and gain a wider audience with whom to share the good news of salvation through Jesus, who bears the name of names! Therefore, I want to thank CSS Publishing for providing me with the opportunity to share the preached word in this printed series of sermons.

My prayer is that God will richly bless those who read these sermons and empower them to "lift high the cross, the love of Christ proclaim" through their witness to the gospel.

Soli Deo Gloria!

Mark J. Molldrem

Foreword

From a purely formal point of view, there is little that is unexpected in this book:
Biblical texts furnish the basis for what is spoken here. For, whoever mounts a pulpit in one place or another can be expected, in one way or another, to make reference to the Bible. Every sermon in this book begins with a biblical text.
Illustrations are used to make clear ideas which would otherwise remain abstract. For, despite the centuries of its exposition at the hands of one genius or another, the ideas in the Bible still need clarifying. Every sermon in this book contains an illustration. For example, in the sermon titled "As Is," our preacher indulges in simile — "like that rusted, yellow Datsun with a cracked head, life breaks down."
There is constant reference in this book to signal characters inside and outside Christian history. For, unless the preacher has given up reading altogether, or lacks interest in the long line of witnesses, it may be assumed that some past or contemporary figure will be leaned on for a bit of help, particularly if that figure says it better than the preacher can. So our pulpiteer cites Saint Augustine, Thomas a Kempis, Toyohiko Kagawa, Soren Kierkegaard, Martin Luther King, Jr., and his namesake. And, unless that preacher has excluded a wider authorship, it may be assumed there will be use of non-theological types, since truth isn't restricted to believers. So our pulpiteer gets a hand up from the old humorist Ambrose Bierce — from which an interest in Lincolnia or the Civil War may be inferred, since (usually) only Civil War buffs know anything about Ambrose Bierce — along with Charles Dickens, Mark Twain, and William Shakespeare.
Not even the titles of the sermons in this book, perhaps the titles least of all, are unique, *sui generis* — "The Righteousness

Of God"; "Obedience"; "New Life From Old"; "Love And Friendship." With possible exceptions (perhaps "Friday — The Good One"), there's hardly anything in the titles to seduce the reader, nothing to equal, say, the title of a sermon on the Baptist once preached by a Dane the Nazis murdered: "Truth Cannot Be Pickled." The titles do not defy exception.

From a purely formal perspective, then, from the purely formal point of view, there's little in this book to evoke our delight or wonder.

Still, there's a uniqueness to this little volume; there's something in it to set it apart, if not from all, at least from most. It's Christocentric, that is, it announces life, liberty, hope, strength, the whole world and every creature in it as originating in, pointing toward, and returning to, Jesus Christ. This little book is perforated, punctuated with talk of Jesus Christ. Now, that is hardly a preoccupation in contemporary preaching, no matter what the denomination. Perhaps because the preaching of Christ involves an exclusion claim athwart political correctness: "No one comes to the Father but by me." Or, perhaps because an age that has set self at the center of its universe naturally tends to begin and end there. At any rate, this volume of sermons however formally similar to others is unlike them due to its continual and everlasting accent on what the Creator has done for the creature in his Holy Child Jesus. It's the preoccupation with Christ, his name, his life and death, his gifts and his power, which sets the book off from its kind. For such a preoccupation, this book deserves reading, and its author our grateful thanks.

Roy A. Harrisville
Emeritus Professor
Luther Seminary
St. Paul, Minnesota

Ash Wednesday   2 Corinthians 5:20b—6:10

The Righteousness Of God

"Hardships ... beatings ... imprisonment ...sleepless nights ... hunger ... in dishonor ... in ill repute ... unknown ... sorrowful ... poor."

It sounds like a street person being described. Wrong! These are word snapshots of the life of the apostle Paul that picture what a follower of Christ must be ready to bear.

Paul was a "street person" of sorts, pounding the pavement in the first century from Jerusalem to Damascus to Rome. His task was not survival, but salvation. Paul preached the salvation from God that comes to all people through Jesus Christ. His invitation was for people to be reconciled to God. His message of how that is accomplished can be summed up in one sentence: "For our sake he made him to be sin who knew no sin, so that in him we might become the righteousness of God."

Sin and righteousness — those are words that can stick in the craw of anyone. Sin! Nobody wants it, though everybody has it. Righteousness! Nobody has it, though everybody wants it.

In recent years it has been difficult to talk publicly about sin. Everyone is a *victim*. No one is really responsible for one's actions. It is someone else in particular or circumstances in general which dictate to a person one's response. Even the *no-fault* language of divorce proceedings abrogates accountability.

This passing the buck should not really surprise us. It is the oldest game on the planet. Adam and Eve invented it in the Garden of Eden. They had been told by God not to eat the fruit of the tree of knowledge of good and evil. They disobeyed. They thought they knew what was right for them. So, rather than listen to God's voice of instruction, they listened to their own voices of desire. When they saw, in the words of the Bible, "that the tree was good for food, and that it was a delight to the eyes, and that the tree was to be desired to make one wise," they took and ate. In direct disobedience to God's command, they followed their own hearts.

When God came looking for them in the cool of the day, they hid. Sin always has a difficulty being out in the open. God asks Adam about his newfound feeling of fear and his awareness of being naked. "Have you eaten of the tree of which I commanded you not to eat?" Adam is quick with his response. "The woman whom you gave to be with me, she gave me fruit from the tree." When God asked Eve about the matter, she was just as quick with her response. "The serpent tricked me." Passing the buck! Nobody wants to be responsible for their choices.

We have learned this game well. All persons know how to make excuses for their actions. There is always a *good reason* for what we do.

"It is because of what happened the other day."

"You made me do it."

"You would have done the same thing, if it had happened to you."

"I'm going through my mid-life crisis."

"It's the alcohol talking."

"Chalk it up to PMS."

One of the fine insights expressed by psychologist Alfred Adler, student of Carl Jung, is that each person is responsible for one's own actions; human beings choose how they respond to any given situation. There may be reasons backing our choices, but it is the individual who makes the final choice.

This places the responsibility where it has always belonged from the beginning of time. "I have sinned," Adam said originally. And we can say that also. As Soren Kierkegaard (nineteenth century Danish theologian) has stated, "How sin came into the world every man understands by himself alone; if he would learn it from another, he *eo ipso* misunderstands it."

With this affirmation, we can understand why "I" is in the middle of "sin." "*Mea culpa*," Augustine would cry. My fault!

We have rebelled against our Commander in Chief on the battlefield of life; we have become the enemy, having deserted our post. Just as there is a court-martial death sentence for such dereliction of duty, there is a spiritual death sentence for those who become enemies of God through their rebellious choices. Paul expresses it this way: "The wages of sin is death ... and so death spread to all because all have sinned."

Will Adam and Eve ever get back into the Garden? Is the flaming sword at the gate to Eden God's last act? Will we ever find peace with God, when our sin stands between us and the sword is drawn over us?

If peace is to come, it will not come by our hand. If reconciliation is to be achieved, we will not be able to negotiate it. We are like a downed airplane, unable to take flight once again on our own.

During World War II, the Kee Bird, a B-29 Flying Fortress, fell out of the sky and belly-flopped in the arctic wasteland of Greenland after it had lost its way on a reconnaissance mission. Just a few years ago, Darryl Greenamyer, who has never been in a plane he could not fly, was given permission to extricate the aircraft from its half-century grave, if he could. He assembled a team and rebuilt the aircraft with cunning ingenuity and perseverance in the arctic freeze. After two years of relentless determination, Greenamyer and his crew got all four engines powered up. They taxied into position and began their history-making attempt to fly the Kee Bird for the first time in five decades. The flight engineer bounced in his seat excitedly. "She wants to fly!" It appeared like it would too, as it approached flight speed, until fire broke out and soon engulfed the plane. The tail section cracked and fell off. For hours the men stood and watched their hopes and dreams go up in smoke. Short of a miracle, the Kee Bird, once down, would never fly again.

Short of a miracle, once fallen in sin, humankind would never take flight with God. The good news that Paul is privileged to announce is that the miracle has happened. God did what we could not do. Through Jesus Christ, God reconciled the world to himself. In Jesus, God exchanged our sin with his righteousness. He gave us what we could not come up with ourselves. The power of Christ's crucifixion on the cross is that the death penalty has been satisfied; the wages of sin have been paid. Though Lent is a reflective season, it really is not a sad time, when we consider what has been accomplished for us and what we are preparing to celebrate.

Just like prisoners get a new set of clothes when they are released from jail, we have been clothed in a new righteousness, the righteousness of God. In his mercy, he has not given us what we deserve for our disobedience — death; by his grace, he has given us what we do not deserve — life. There is new life for anyone who has been grounded by the gravity of sin. God will see to it. God will give it. It is his right to do so. It is his righteousness to do so.

The marks of this new life, reconciled to God, are peace, joy, hope, and purpose. Here we come back to Paul's description of life as a servant of God, as outlined in our text. In the midst of the trials of life as a Christian, God grants blessings that help us rise above the crash sites of our daily lives: joy in sorrow, contentment in poverty, integrity in the face of lies, strength in weakness.

The ashes of this day remind us that we have crash-landed and will not rise up again on our own. These same ashes, as they are shaped into the cross on our foreheads, remind us of how Jesus has come to the crash site of our humanity. He enters into our sinfulness in such a way as to take it upon himself and give us his righteousness in exchange. His righteousness is to forgive, as he said from the cross, "Father, forgive them." His righteousness is to reopen the gate to the Garden, "Today, you will be with me in paradise." The flaming sword against the sin is replaced by his burning love for the sinner.

During this season of Lent, let us reflect gratefully on the unsurpassable gift of love God has given us through Jesus Christ, who reconciled us to God, setting aside the penalty for our sins and forgiving us into a state of new life with him. Let us be encouraged to live faithfully, so that we, by anything we say or do, would not place any obstacle in the way for another person to believe in the goodness of God through Jesus Christ. Amen.

Lent 1 1 Peter 3:18-22

Adoption Into God's Family

Any parent who has adopted a child knows the joy of bringing a new member into the family. There is joy in the heart of our Heavenly Father when someone is baptized into his family. Baptism is like adoption.

There are many children orphaned from the love of a family. Teenage pregnancies, unwanted children, unfit parents who abuse or desert their children, even unexpected death: These tragedies leave many children orphaned from the love of a family.

Thank God there are people who want to be parents and for many different reasons are willing to adopt a love-orphaned child into their own family. They will approach the social service and court system to make their appeal. Applications need to be filled out. Numerous interviews and a careful scrutinizing of their lives take place. Expensive costs are paid. There are two, three, maybe more court hearings. A probationary period follows.

Then, there are the questions that cascade over the whole process. Do we have the right credentials? Has everything been done right? Will the request be granted? Will the child be ours to love and raise? Will the child grow to love us? Many anxious moments are filled with doubts and hopes. Finally, the words come from the judge: "Yes! Granted! All the requirements have been fulfilled. The child shall be claimed yours."

There is joy in the family now. The first step has been accomplished. Everyone is so thankful. What an even more beautiful child now! Life begins in a new way all over again in the family.

First there is the new name, the family name, that graces the child, proudly to be spoken to the rest of the family and friends. Then, there are the tasks of daily love: washing, feeding, clothing, teaching, disciplining, playing, protecting, watching, listening, sharing — all the things that make for caring.

In such an adoptive love the child grows, knowing who he or she is as part of the family, loved from moments of helplessness and hopelessness through time with the family to moments of hopefulness and helpfulness. Placed on the parents' insurance policies and in the family will, the child becomes an inheritor of the family treasures by virtue of the adoption.

Baptism is like adoption.

All children, all people are orphans in a world of sin. Adam and Eve are our first parents. In its pride and self-centered rebellion against God, the human family has become tragically separated. We have all been orphaned outside of the family garden. *Our pride and self-centered rebellion against God prove that we are children of darkness, a no-people with no bond of love between us that will let us live together gracefully, no bond of love that will let us live before God rightfully.* Orphans in the dark world of sin — that is who we are and that is who we would still be, if it were not for the infinite love of our Heavenly Father, who desires us to be children of the light, members of his family of love.

The Heavenly Father approaches our human system to make his appeal. He goes through the requirements. In Jesus Christ, the heaven-sent Son, God became like us in every respect. The Son gave up the glory of the Father, so that he might fully identify with the very people he wished to bring into his family. He became like us, so that we might know and understand the very Father who desires us all to be his children.

Like any adoption proceedings, there is a cost to be paid. In our courts, there are human factors to be dealt with and money helps cover the debts. But between the heart of God and the hearts of men, women, and children there are spiritual factors to be dealt with. Here, silver and gold are of no value. "The wages of sin is death," the Law reminds us. Because we are orphaned in sin, the debt must be paid with death.

Here is where the love of the Father is seen at its greatest. In Jesus Christ, the Father accepts the wage, the debt. Jesus Christ loves us to death, literally he loves us to death on a cross. Martin Luther in his Small Catechism puts it this way in explanation of the Second Article of the Apostles' Creed: "At great cost he has [adopted me], a lost and [orphaned child], not with silver and gold but with his holy and precious blood and his innocent suffering and death." Paul writes in Galatians, "But when the fullness of time had come, God sent his Son, born of a woman, born under the law, in order to redeem those who were under the law, so that we might receive adoption as children."

The anxious moments of sin, the fear of our own guilt and death are all drowned, as it were. For the claim has been made by God, the Father himself, judge of the universe, that we shall be his, children of his loving heart and family. This is done in baptism. It is our adoption as sons and daughters.

Paul writes, "We were buried with him by baptism into death." The wages of sin have been paid. The way has been cleared and the law satisfied. As we are united with Christ through baptism, we are adopted sons and daughters of God, our Father in heaven. Peter expresses it this way: "For Christ also suffered for sins once for all, the righteous for the unrighteous, in order to bring you to God."

What joy there is in heaven! The first step has been accomplished. To paraphrase Peter's words, "Once we were no people, but now we are God's people; once we had not received mercy, but now we have received mercy; once we were orphaned in sin, but now we are adopted in love." And life begins in a new way all over again in the family.

First there is the new name: child of God, Christian, the family's name, proudly to be spoken to the rest of the family and friends and world. Then, there are the tasks of daily love: the daily washing as we repent of our sins and return to our baptism, the feeding at the family meal of Holy Communion to nourish us for life's journey, the clothing in the righteousness of Christ to guard us from the evil one, the teaching from the Word, the disciplining for maturing in Christ, the playing of the Spirit on our hope-filled imaginations, the protecting of the Father of mercies, the watching, listening, sharing of the family together in Christ-like caring.

In such an adoptive love the baptized person grows, knowing who he or she is as part of the family, loved right out of being an orphan to share in the inheritance of the family treasures. These treasures are the forgiveness of sin, deliverance from death and the devil, and life everlasting.

If a person knows nothing else than this, if a person knows nothing else of God than this — what is learned in baptism — it is enough. Here is wisdom that far surpasses human knowledge. Here is a work of God that is far more effective than any human work.

The one who has been baptized can know that "God loves you." The Heavenly Father was willing to go to any extent, even the death of his Son, to have you adopted into his family. This privilege is not yours by right of birth. By birth you are a creature of God, but orphaned by sin and outside the family of God. In baptism you are adopted into the family. The relationship is changed. You are now children of the Heavenly Father with other brothers and sisters to Jesus himself in this family of love.

A seven-year-old boy tugged at the sleeve of his new adopting father as they were leaving the courtroom, where the final papers had just been signed. "I love you," the boy said. "Thank you," the new father said, and added, "but in these past several months during all these proceedings you never once said that. How come now?"

The boy responded, "You have signed your name on the judge's paper. You gave me your name. You really did adopt me. Now I know you love me." And they walked into the rest of their family life together hand in hand.

That is you, child of God, adopted in your baptism by your loving Heavenly Father. Walk hand in hand with him into the rest of your life. Amen.

Lent 2　　　　　　　　　　　　　　　Romans 4:13-25

The Gospel
Of Our Calling

A friend related to me how, when he was a youngster, he spent a lot of time on the other side of the block all wrapped up in touch football and whiffle ball and hide-and-go-seek. But there were other important events going on for which his folks knew he needed to be present, like going to church, mealtime, bedtime. So, they blew a whistle to call him home from the other side of the block.

God also calls, not with a whistle, but with his Word. Martin Luther in his Small Catechism explains the Third Article of the Apostles' Creed in this way: "I believe that I cannot by my own understanding or effort believe in Jesus Christ my Lord or come to him, but the Holy Spirit calls me through the gospel...." *The Gospel of our calling!*

It is so easy for us to get all wrapped up in the affairs of our own making. Not just football, whiffle ball, or hide-and-go-seek, but also work — that can leave so little time for anything or anyone else; and relaxation from work — that can leave little or no time for worship or community service.

It is so easy to get all wrapped up in the affairs of our own making. Intrigue with friends and neighbors can pit one against another for position of power and influence, who was right and who was wrong. These local misadventures are escalated on a larger scale between nations. More than one bad turn of fortune in our personal lives and we can begin the downward spiral of despair, thinking life is not fair and no one is for us and what's the use of it all. We can get sick and give up on God and on ourselves. From such daily distractions we need to be called to more important events going on.

And so, God calls us, as no one else can do. He called Abraham from out of his daily routines in Ur to risk a journey into the future. His only "chart and compass" for this journey would be the promises of God. God promised Abraham that he would give him a new land, and from him to make a new nation, and through him to bless the entire world. Abraham listened to God's call and responded. His response is called faith, for he rested not on what he could see or create himself, but solely on the promises of God.

Like Abraham, God calls us today. The land, the nation, and the blessing have already been given. Now, God has more promises to keep to those who will have faith and trust him. God calls us into these promises, not with a whistle, but with his Word.

God's Word, as expressed in one of John's letters, is that "if we confess our sins, he who is faithful and just will forgive our sins and cleanse us from all unrighteousness." That is a promise. God calls us into the forgiveness of sins! It is this call into the forgiveness of sins that makes Christianity distinctly what it is. Paul writes that Jesus was "handed over to death for our trespasses and was raised for our justification." We have a problem that stands between us and God. That problem is sin. Sin has to be dealt with or we will forever be separated from God, alienated by our rebelliousness, like wayward children are from loving parents.

There is only one resolution for this problem. God has to do something to heal the breach. We are not capable of doing it, just like Abraham and Sarah could not bear children in their old age. We are as good as dead in our sin, barren in our relationship with God. If our sin is to be overcome, it will have to be overcome by God, who said through the prophet Jeremiah, "I will forgive their iniquity, and remember their sin no more."

God is able to do what he promises. In Jesus, God fleshed out his love and extended his hand of mercy. On the cross, Jesus offered the words that cover a multitude of sins when he said, "Father, forgive them."

Without the forgiveness of sins, we are no people; we have no calling; we are left on the other side of the block. With the forgiveness of sins, we are a people; we have a calling; we are brought home. As Peter writes, "Once you were no people, but now you are God's people; once you had not received mercy, but now you have received mercy, that you may declare the wonderful deeds of him who called you out of darkness into his marvelous light."

Rhonda was a beautiful nineteen-year-old coed who had become infatuated with one of her professors. She succumbed to the temptation of spending several nights with him. While this was going on, she was uneasy. She knew she had violated her own standards of conduct and she had a growing sense of having violated God's will in this passing relationship.

She sought counsel because her guilt was getting in the way of how she felt about herself. She was becoming depressed and unable to do her schoolwork well. She was drinking excessively, and was on edge with every member of her family.

Rhonda was a Christian. She turned to God for forgiveness, but seemed unable to find assurance that her sins were indeed forgiven once she had confessed them honestly to God. The counselor led Rhonda to the fifth chapter of Romans where she encountered such words as these: "God shows his love for us in that while we were yet sinners Christ died for us."

Rhonda read on and discovered herself in the words of Scripture. God can and did indeed forgive her sins. It was offered even while she was sinning — in fact, way before! She found release from her guilt and was assured of God's forgiveness. She could look at herself in the morning with a smile on her face. Her family saw the difference and home-life improved. She confronted her teacher with her newfound faith and broke off the relationship.

God calls us in our fractured, guilt-ridden world of day-to-day mis-living. He calls us with Good News: ***The Gospel of our calling into the forgiveness of sins.***

When Paul was in prison, he wrote a letter to his Christian friends in Philippi. In this letter he made the statement that "living is Christ and dying is gain." He went on to explain that although he needed to remain alive in order to carry on his ministry, he would prefer "to depart and be with Christ," as he put it, "for that is far better." Then, later he says, "I press on toward the goal for the prize of the heavenly call of God in Christ Jesus." Notice the direction of this call: the prize of the *heavenly* call.

One of the undeniable aspects of our Christian faith, of our Christian calling, is that of eternal life. There is an everlasting blessedness that awaits each and every one who trusts in God through Jesus Christ. Peter speaks of this as "the hope that is in you."

One of the expectations of the Lenten season is to arrive at Easter Sunday and celebrate the resurrection of Jesus Christ. Because of what Jesus has done for us and ahead of us, we are confident that life eternal awaits the believer beyond the gates of death.

The Boston Marathon is run every year. A marathon is a distance run of 26 miles. It tests the stamina of each participant. At the finish line the winner is given a laurel wreath to crown his sweated brow. Have you noticed how the winners run with head erect and eyes forward? "I press on toward the goal." The runners always keep in mind the finish line. It helps give them the courage to keep putting one foot in front of the other, step by step, stride by stride to the completion of the race and the laurel wreath. In the Book of Revelation we read: "Be faithful unto death and I will give you the crown of life." For the Christian who runs the distance of life in faith, there awaits eternal life to crown the sweated brow.

God calls us in our fainting, tiring, mortal day-to-day living. He calls us with Good News: **The Gospel of our calling into everlasting life.**

This is not only a tremendous comfort in time of grief and sorrow; it is also the very sum and substance of meaningful living today. This hope of our calling to life everlasting is our very strength and drive for living a purposeful and energetic life now — step by step, stride by stride to the finish line.

C.S. Lewis, that great English convert to Christianity, comments that "we are [not] to leave the present world as it is. If you read history you will find that the Christians who did most for the present world were just those who thought most of the next." Now the list would be long, but just consider these heavenly-minded people: the apostles, who set a fire for conversion across the entire Roman empire that changed the lives of kings and princes, peddlers and paupers; Martin Luther, who changed the church around in the sixteenth century; John Wesley, who fought the political system of England on behalf of the poor — and won; the English Evangelical Christians, who abolished the slave trade in the British Empire long before the new America began to think about it. You see, just because we are heavenly-minded does not mean that we are no earthly good. Quite the contrary!

You have been called in the forgiveness of sins to life everlasting. It is a gift that comes to you through Baptism to claim you by the grace of God, so that you might know who you are and whose you are as children of the Heavenly Father.

You have been called in the forgiveness of sins to life everlasting. It is a gift that comes to you through Holy Communion to strengthen you by the grace of God time and again for life's journey.

You have been called in the forgiveness of sins to life everlasting. It is a gift that comes to you through the preached Word by the grace of God to give you a vision of your life in the whole of things, human and divine.

When God calls, listen and believe. Amen.

Lent 3   1 Corinthians 1:18-25

The Word Of The Cross Is The Power of God

When Neil Armstrong was on the moon, an American flag was planted to signify the accomplishment of his journey. The goal had been established in 1960 to set a man on the moon before the end of the decade. In 1969, that goal was achieved in a most dramatic way.

When Jesus was on the earth, he planted a cross to signify the accomplishment of his journey. The goal had been established from the foundation of the world that God would love the world, no matter what it took. On a place called The Skull during the Roman occupation of Palestine, that goal was achieved in a most dramatic way.

The cross is a sign that the journey is ended, the destination has been achieved, the work is accomplished. "It is finished," Jesus said from the cross. The Word from God is the word of the cross.

Pierre Chardin, Christian author and observer of the world, has written, "The human epic resembles nothing so much as a way of the cross." Any casual observer of humanity will recognize that every cradle swings over an open grave. We place crosses on graves.

We have crosses to bear. There are diseases and illnesses that stalk us, seeking to nail us on the scaffold of pain and fear. There are relationships that, though they are important to us, die a thousand deaths because of our ineptitude at really caring for one another. We have hopes and dreams that go to sleep with the night and never awaken with the new day's light. We may desire to live on high ground under sunny skies, but we cannot avoid walking through the valley of the shadows.

It is not bright and cheerful to talk about crosses. It is much more comfortable talking about commonplace sorts of things that warm the heart: caressing a baby, drying clothes on the line in a gentle spring breeze, getting out into the fields to turn the earth once again and plant the crops, celebrating birthdays and anniversaries, visiting with friends over a cup of coffee, canoeing down a meandering river, laughing with children.

The word of the cross? We would rather not hear it. Rather not, but yet we do. We cannot avoid it. Nor can we avoid the figure of Jesus. In the midst of our cross-strewn ways, he comes, carrying his cross and being hung upon it. This haunts us. We cannot sidestep the specter of this One, who intended only good for all, yet was crucified as a common criminal. He willingly took his cross, letting the worst happen to himself, yet trusted in his Heavenly Father to make something of it. He prayed in the Garden, "Not my will, but yours be done." In the word of the cross, can the power of God be present? It seems a bit like folly.

On the cross so many years ago, Jesus cried out, "My God, my God, why have you forsaken me?" These are pounding words from the cross about the cross that echo the deep feelings in our hearts when we too have felt forsaken. What is it about the word of the cross that keeps reverberating through time? Cross-bearers like us, when we hear this word of the cross, our ears perk up and we are attentive. Why is that?

Think of the oyster. It is a clammy, cold, ugly mollusk. Lying on the ocean floor, it is subject to the intrusion of a grain of sand — an irritation in the seemingly complacent life of the oyster. By not ignoring the painful intrusion or waiting for it to go away, but by paying special attention to it and surrounding it with its own secretions, the oyster creates the pearl — a treasure of beauty and worth.

Jesus said that the kingdom of heaven is like a merchant in search of fine pearls, who, on finding one pearl of great value, went and sold all that he had and bought it. Imagine, a grain of sand becoming so important.

The word of the cross! Imagine, it becomes so important, a treasure of beauty and worth. Despite its ugly appearance, and its nature of intruding upon our lives as we would like to live them — could there be here a pearl of great worth that would warrant selling all that we own and investing in it?

The word of the cross is the pearl of God, the power of God. For at the center of every one of the crosses that we bear in life is *the* cross of Jesus Christ.

Jesus, the bringer of God's love to the world, died on the cross. God used that apparent defeat to demonstrate his very *power* over life and death and all the forces of evil. Hidden in weakness, God enticed the evils of this world to nail Jesus on the cross and then in the moment of their seeming victory, he clutched them to himself and drew them into the grave with him. There he dealt them a death blow that brought their power to an end.

Because of that one singular cross upon which Christ died once for all, the power of God is at hand to help everyone to bear their crosses. That pearl of infinite worth can belong to anyone by faith. Faith finds the power of God in the word of the cross. The power of God *is* the word of the cross. God took what was foolish and weak in the world and made it into a standard of strength for all who believe.

When life takes on a clammy, cold and ugly appearance, do not forget the oyster and how to look for the treasure inside. When life brings you crosses to bear, do not forget the cross of Christ. It is the power of God to lead you through suffering with patience, character, and hope which will not disappoint you.

Vernon Bittner, in his book *Make Your Illness Count*, talks about how an illness or a tragedy can be a stepping stone to greater living. That was certainly true for Gordon Gund. In his early thirties, his eyesight gave way to a disease. Blind and visionless, he despaired. As his family rallied around him, he began to look deep inside himself. Finally, he applied himself with the gifts that God had given him. He remade his life. He became the owner of the Cleveland Cavaliers of the National Basketball Association and has established a foundation for eye research.

If we want, we can learn about ourselves, we can truly see other people, and we can grow in faith, hope, and love — if we pay attention to our crosses and learn to find the treasure in the midst of it all. The treasure for the Christian is the love of God in Jesus Christ who is with us, hidden in the shape of crosses, helping us grow into real, eyes-wide-open, caring, loving, thankful human beings.

The word of the cross is the power of God!

Martin Luther, in his delicious treatise *The Magnificat*, expresses it this way: "God will continue to let his people become powerless, and to be brought low, until everyone supposes their end is near. Yet in these very things he is present to them with all his power. He hides himself in the cross with those who suffer. Only faith can see this. Here is the fulness of God's power and his outstretched arm. For where man's strength ends, God's strength begins. When the suffering comes to an end, it will be apparent what great strength was hidden underneath the weakness. In the same way Christ was powerless on the cross; yet there he performed his mightiest work. He defeated and conquered sin, death, world, hell, devil and all evil for you."[1]

Wow! Fellow cross-bearers, as you bear your cross on life's journey, hear the word of the cross. Take heart and be of courage. See Jesus! Believe in Jesus! He bore his cross for all for the forgiveness of sins and for life everlasting. The word of the cross is the power of God and the power of God is the word of the cross, on which God has brought you life abundant and life eternal. Amen.

---

1. Reprinted from *The Magnificat: Luther's Commentary*, translated by A. T. W. Steinhauser, copyright © 1967 Augsburg Publishing House. Used by permission.

Lent 4　　　　　　　　　　　　　　Ephesians 2:1-10

As Is

Once upon a long time ago, a friend of mine owned a yellow Datsun. It was a neat little car that took him over the hills and through the valleys of southern Wisconsin. With "five on the floor," it was fun to drive, shifting up and down, turning left and right, accelerating and stepping on the breaks. The yellow Datsun kept him happy for a couple years, until one day it died. The head cracked and the engine decided not to turn over any longer. It was a sad day for my friend, his only consolation coming from the farmer who was willing to buy it for $200 *as is*. He figured he could fix it and provide his son with a runabout. More power to him! My friend could not fix it; that was not his skill or interest. He was happy just to get $200 *as is* for the now rusted, yellow Datsun with no power.

The second law of thermodynamics talks about the natural and eventual decay of matter. "What's the matter with my Datsun?" my friend had cried when it broke down. The matter with the Datsun was that it was matter. Although matter has its day, in time it will only decay. There are limitations built into the very fabric of things. How disappointing that may be! Yet, how gratifying that there was one person who was willing to take the defunct Datsun *as is*.

Life, like that bright, yellow Datsun, certainly has its day. There are times when everything seems to come together and we are so happy. But, life does not stay that way. Like that rusted, yellow Datsun with a cracked head, life breaks down. It sputters along and eventually dies. Like the second law of thermodynamics, our life, as much as we want it to be upward and onward, instead decays. It happens a little bit today; then, more tomorrow.

We can look at our lives and see how many ways in which we are broken. We do not measure up to what we would like from ourselves. We have dreams, but they often turn into nightmares. We have an image of ourselves, but it is tarnished. We know the truth of the words, "You were dead through the trespasses and sins in which you once lived, following the course of this world." Paul expresses this in another way in his Letter to the Romans: "There is no distinction ... all have sinned and fall short of the glory of God."

It is amazing that Christians and seekers keep coming to a place of worship called the House of God. It is more like a junkyard of human Datsuns. We are humble enough to admit that. We begin our worship with the confession of our sins. We admit that we are captive to sin and are not able to free ourselves. We have sinned against God in thought, word, and deed. This happens by the evil we do and the good we leave undone. We do not love God with our whole heart, like the writer of Deuteronomy prescribes for us: "You shall love the Lord your God with all your heart, and with all your soul, and with all your might." We do not love our neighbors as ourselves. Rusted with a cracked head, we are going nowhere. This is who we are. This is as we are. And we cannot fix ourselves. It is a law.

What is to become of us? My friend was ready to junk his Datsun. But, then, this farmer came along and bought it *as is*. He was willing to pay the price to give that car a second chance.

The writer to the Ephesians explains that we — broken, bent, rusted, and cracked — are saved by grace. This is not our own doing; it is a gift from God.

There is a word in the New Testament that speaks of this. That word is *redeem*. It is a term that comes from the slave market. In days of old, slaves were brought into the public square and auctioned off. Certain buyers would bid for them, pay the price, and then set the slave free. The slave was redeemed from the auction block, bought and freed, given a new life. Oftentimes, former slaves would go to work as free persons for the benefactors who had redeemed them.

Just like that farmer redeemed the yellow Datsun from the scrap heap, so too God redeems us from hell and a life separated from God. God does this through Jesus Christ. For God so loved the world, that he sent his only Son ... who accepts us *as is*, or as the reformer Martin Luther would say, "With warts and all." This gracious act of God gives us new life.

This new life is described in these words of scripture: "God, who is rich in mercy, out of the great love with which he loved us even when we were dead through our trespasses, made us alive together with Christ — by grace you have been saved — and raised us up with him and seated us with him in the heavenly places in Christ Jesus."

Yes, we fall short of the glory of God. But, God's love is so great that God is willing to take us *as is*. That is grace; that is "the gift of God."

Now, if you have gotten in the habit of getting down on yourself, you are just going to have to stop doing that. Not because you do not have reason to get down on yourself. We all have plenty of spilled milk to cry over. But, God does a new thing with us and we better wake up to it. God takes us *as is* and loves us, just as we are.

Some people need guilt to motivate them to do good. They know they have done something wrong; so, out of guilt they try to do three or four good things to compensate, in order to make up for it. Then, they think they are leading a pretty good life. Sorry, that just does not work! Try it. You are always left with the nagging question, "Is it enough?" Can we ever be sure that we have done enough good to offset the bad that we have done? Honestly, do we not find with the writer of Ecclesiastes that a little evil outweighs a lot of good? We can never be sure that we have done enough to balance out the shortfalls in our lives.

Paul rightfully says that all have sinned and fall short of the glory of God. Then, he truthfully adds that we can be set right with God only by his grace as a gift: *as is*.

To live by faith is to accept God at his word. When he says he loves us, while we were yet sinners, believe him and be loved *as is*.

Of course, do not expect to remain the same. The Bible reminds us over and over again to love *as* we have been loved, to forgive *as* we have been forgiven, to do good unto others *as* God has done good to us. "For we are what he has made us, created in Christ Jesus for good works, which God prepared beforehand to be our way of life."

When it finally dawned upon Kurt that God loved him in spite of his criminal behavior, he stopped stealing and beating people up; he started for the first time in his life to look for ways to help his neighbors. When Joan realized that God was able to love her even when she was having an affair with her best friend's husband, she turned her guilt over to such a love, stopped the affair, and discovered a new, more lasting joy in her life. When Alex accepted that his life was totally out of control and that his suicide attempt had failed, he turned his life over to the care of God *as is* and experienced a rebirth of his spirit. Now, he works at a crisis center, helping youth deal with their endless problems.

God takes you as you are; then he works on you and works in you and works with you to make you into what he wills you to be — up and running in a new way. You may be a yellow Datsun; that is nothing to boast about. But, you are also a redeemed child of God; that is something to rejoice in. Amen.

Lent 5   Hebrews 5:5-10

Prayer Clothes

Going to northern Canada? Bring your parka.
Going to the pool? Do not forget your swimsuit.
Going to the big game? Put on school colors.
Going to the beach? You better remember the sunscreen.

It is important to know where you are going. Then, you will know what to wear.

Jesus was going to die. So, he wrapped himself in prayer. Throughout the gospel accounts we see Jesus praying, whether with his disciples or alone. Like a priest who offers prayers for the people and himself, Jesus "offered up prayers and supplications" to his Heavenly Father. Well-practiced in prayer, it should come as no surprise that Jesus is the one to whom the disciples turned when they wanted to learn how to pray. To that particular request, Jesus taught them the Lord's Prayer, which has been handed down to us today: "Our Father, who art in heaven...."

Jesus was going to die. There is no place in the scriptures where Jesus is more focused in prayer over his future than when he is in the Garden of Gethsemane on the eve of his crucifixion. Surely it was this singular experience to which the writer to the Hebrews refers with these words, "In the days of his flesh, Jesus offered up prayers and supplications, with loud cries and tears, to the one who was able to save him from death, and he was heard because of his reverent submission." In Gethsemane we find Jesus clothed in prayer. Jesus is grieved and agitated, so he covers himself in prayer. The future is before him, but the silhouette of a cross looks so bloody and bleak. So, to get from here to there, Jesus prays.

Prayer is the bridge that Jesus builds in order to talk with his Heavenly Father. The Latin word for "priest" is *pontifex*, which means "bridge builder." Jesus is described in the Letter to the Hebrews as "a high priest according to the order of Melchizedek." As a priest, Jesus builds a bridge of prayer between heaven and earth. He crosses that bridge not once, not twice, but three times in that short span of time in the Garden of Gethsemane, as the future stared him straight in the face and straight through his heart.

Getting his will in line with the will of his Heavenly Father was so important to Jesus that he invested his last hours as a free man on his knees. He wore prayer like a comfortable flannel shirt. Jesus understood how important it was to be in conversation with his Heavenly Father, if he were to take any steps forward into his future. Three times he prayed in the garden, searching for that perfect union of wills.

The number three is often used in the Bible to express completeness. Jesus was given three precious gifts by the Magi who had come to worship him. Jesus was tempted three times in the wilderness and three times he defeated the Devil's trickery. The gospel writer Matthew reports Jesus telling his disciples on three separate occasions about his impending suffering and death. Jesus is in the grave three days. What Jesus experiences in worship, in temptation, in suffering and death *is complete*. When Jesus prays three times to his Heavenly Father, he is completely in prayer. For he knows that is the only way he can get from Gethsemane to Golgotha.

Notice the content of Jesus' prayer. It is not about himself. It is about the will of God. "My Father, if it is possible, let this cup pass from me; yet not what I want but what you want." And again, "My Father, if this cannot pass unless I drink it, your will be done." Jesus wanted only to put his life in line with the will of God. If it be God's will that Jesus suffer and die for the sins of the world, so be it. It will be hard, yes. But it will not be impossible; for with God all things are possible.

It is God's will that accomplishes what God wills to accomplish.

When God desired to create a world, he stepped out into space and willed the world into being by the power of his word. "Let there be light." And there was light.

When God desired to free a people from slavery in Egypt, he stepped onto the stage of history and willed it so. "Let my people go." And they went.

When God desired to save the world that had turned its back on him, he found a manger and a way to make visible the very love of his heart. "For a child has been born for us." And the Word became flesh.

Jesus knew that to go anywhere with his life or even for his death to have any meaning, it would be important to be in sync with his Heavenly Father, who is able to accomplish what he wills to accomplish. Therefore, not my will, but yours be done, he prayed.

Jesus literally prayed his way into the future. Even when that future looked gory and grim, when Golgotha and the specter of crucifixion lay in front of him, he lined up his life with his Heavenly Father's vision for him.

The Father's vision for him was this: that God loved the world so much that he sent his Son, as Paul expressed it, to die for the ungodly, to redeem those under the law, so that we might receive adoption as children of God. Life will come through death; a resurrection will come after crucifixion.

Jesus had to accept his cruel and painful death as the means by which God would save the world. Jesus had to surrender his will over to the will of his Heavenly Father. He prayed his way from here to there. Jesus bridged his present to the future with prayer. He prayed his way into the future. Jesus himself followed the advice of scripture, where it says in the Psalms, "As for me, I will call upon God; and the Lord shall save me. Evening, and morning, and at noon, will I pray."

Now the question for you is: How do you get from here to there? How do you find your way into the future? Are you going into the future? Maybe the prospects don't look that encouraging to you, just like they did not look encouraging to Jesus.

Are you concerned about your health, your very life? Does aging have its grip on you? Is there a medical prognosis that casts the shadow of a cross over you?

Do you have financial struggles, either because you have too little or because you want too much? Is money becoming the driving value in your life, determining the decisions you make? Is your anxiety over the things of this world?

Do relationships bring you heartache? Have people disappointed you and hurt you? Do you find family and friends drifting outside of your sphere of influence?

Has work lost its meaning? Or have you lost your work? Do you wonder what to do with your life in terms of any meaningful enterprise, either in employment or in retirement?

There are real, human situations with which to wrestle. Jesus wrestled in the Garden, but not alone. He teaches us how to get from here to there; he shows us how to pray our way into the future. We do not know what the future holds, but we know who holds the future. With our prayers, like Jesus did, we can place our lives in the hands of God.

Prayer is built on the premise that God has a will for our lives. Prayer prepares us to receive that will and live according to it. Prayer empowers us to be the people God wants us to be.

In prayer we are in the presence of our Heavenly Father. *Just as* he was with his Son, Jesus, all the way to the cross and into the grave and then most gloriously beyond the grave into new life, *just so* he will be with you.

There is no garden so far removed that your Heavenly Father cannot find you in prayer. There is no bedroom so dark or tear-stained that your Heavenly Father cannot comfort you in prayer. There is no burden so crushing that your Heavenly Father cannot lift you up in prayer. There is no future so impossible that your Heavenly Father cannot lead you there according to his will.

"Prayer is an invitation to God to intervene in our lives, to let His will prevail in our affairs," according to Abraham Joshua Heschel.

Let prayer clothe you with a desire only to do the will of your Heavenly Father. It is the best way to get from here to there. It is how your future can be addressed and dressed most perfectly. Amen.

Passion/Palm Sunday   Philippians 2:5-11

Obedience

Sunday was a day in Jesus' life that started the week off with palms and praises — a week that ended with persecution and passion.

Today is a strange day. I do not know if I should be happy or sad. If I were with the crowd on that first Palm Sunday, I think I would be happy, publicly shouting the praises of Jesus as he came riding into Jerusalem. If I knew at that time what the rest of the week would bring, I think I would be sad, knowing that Jesus would end up on a cross and buried in a borrowed tomb.

It is a strange day. Should I celebrate? Or should I weep? Maybe what I should do is not ask questions of myself, but ask questions of Jesus. He is, after all, the central figure in the entire drama of Holy Week. What is Jesus about at this time in his life? Did he feel like celebrating? Did he feel like weeping? Were the palms or was the passion most on his mind?

In the gospel accounts of Matthew, Mark, and Luke, there are conversations of Jesus recorded before Holy Week, conversations that predict his tragic crucifixion. Jesus knew what awaited him in Jerusalem; yet, as the Scripture says, "He set his face to go to Jerusalem." Jesus had been given a mission in life and he would be faithful to that mission; he would be obedient to the will of God.

Paul also writes this about Jesus, in what some have described as the Christ hymn of the early church. Paul describes Jesus as emptying himself of his heavenly glory and taking the form of a servant. Jesus is born on earth; he humbles himself and becomes obedient unto death, even death on a cross. Jesus, the Son of God, accepts the death sentence, so that we might have life. Remember that he died because of our sin. Paul writes this truth elsewhere, that "the wages of sin is death."

Personally, this is what it means: I am a sinner, therefore I must die for my sins. My blood is the price I must pay for my rebellion against God, like Ceausescu paid for his sins against the Romanian people. The problem is that once I have paid for my sins, I am dead, finished, no more. God, not wanting me to perish, sent his son to pay the price for me. He shed his blood and died in my place, for my sins, that I might have life in his name. As that gospel verse within the Gospel of John expresses it: "For God so loved the world that he gave his only Son, so that everyone who believes in him may not perish but may have eternal life."

Jesus' mission was to pay the price of sin. He knew that the price would be his own life, his own blood. Yet, he did not turn aside from his mission. He was obedient, as Paul writes, "Obedient to the point of death — even death on a cross."

There certainly were opportunities for Jesus to back out of his mission. He could have avoided Jerusalem altogether, simply not have gone there. He could have headed to the hills of Judea or up into the back country of Galilee and lived out his days in peace and quiet. He did not. He was obedient.

When he entered Jerusalem and the crowds welcomed him with palms and praises, he could have excited them to revolt against the Romans and also the established religious order of Jerusalem. In this way, he could set up his own little kingdom. He did not. He was obedient.

After Sunday's parade when things quieted down and he started to realize that the masses would not follow him into the Garden of Gethsemane and through the trial and onto Golgotha, he could have slipped out of town and set up his own commune of faithful, though few followers. The Essenes did this, living in the wilderness, separated from society while they waited for the day of judgment. He did not. He was obedient.

On Thursday evening, when he went to the garden to pray, he could have told his Heavenly Father that enough was enough. "You cannot expect me to do this, Father. It is beyond my capabilities. I would rather continue my mission in another way. Let's see if something else would work to bring your people back to you." No! He did not. He prayed instead, "Not my will but yours be done." He was obedient.

When they came to arrest him in the garden, one of his disciples drew a sword and attacked, cutting off someone's ear. But Jesus said that if he wanted he could have called to his Heavenly Father for twelve legions of angels to come and deliver him. He did not. He was obedient.

In the trials that followed throughout the night on into the early morning, Jesus had opportunity to renounce his mission and do obeisance to Caesar. That would have put an end to it. "Not guilty." He would have been set free as a loyal citizen of Rome. He did not. He was obedient.

On the cross he could have given up in despair, cursed his tormentors, cursed God for deserting him, and cursed himself for being so stupid as to get himself into this mess. He did not. He was obedient.

To the very end, Jesus was obedient to his mission. In his last dying words he forgave those who killed him and he committed his spirit into God's loving hands, which he believed were there for him even in the darkness of that afternoon.

There were so many opportunities for Jesus to back out of his mission to die for the sins of the world. He did not. He was obedient, "obedient to the point of death — even death on a cross."

During Holy Week we are called to pay attention to the work that Jesus accomplished for us. He said on the cross, "It is finished." The parade is over. The trial is completed. The execution is final. The wage has been paid. What now?

You have heard these events. You are witnesses. Now, the Holy Spirit is calling upon the witnesses of these events to believe. Accept that Jesus was obedient unto death, even death on a cross *for you.* So much does God love you that he sent his only Son to die on the cross for your sins. A fellow sinner by the name of Paul writes, "God proves his love for us in that while we still were sinners Christ died for us." *This* is what Jesus was all about.

We who are witnesses to these events are called upon to live our lives one holy week after another. Every week is holy when it celebrates the triumphal entry of Jesus in our hearts. Every week is holy when it is lived under the shadow of the cross. From palms to passion, from joy to sorrow, every week of our lives can be wrapped in the love of God, when we live each day of the week in the name of Jesus Christ our Lord, who was obedient to the point of death — even death on a cross *for you* and *for all.* Amen.

Good Friday   Hebrews 10:16-25

Friday —
The Good One

A youngster in Sunday School asked the pastor, "If Jesus died on Friday, why do we call it good?"

It seems contrary to reason to call this day *Good* Friday, when congregations around the world remember Jesus' death with black and an empty chancel. Images like these recount the day: forsaken, scorn, thorns, despised, grief, sorrow, wounded, tears, darkness, and death. How can we use a word like *good* in the same breath? What good can come from Jesus' death on the cross on a day long ago on a hill called "the place of the skull"?

Several years ago Granger Westberg wrote his classic book *Good Grief*. He explained how grief was a normal and necessary human experience at a time of loss. Healthy people engage their sorrow and work through it in such a way so as to emerge from their valley of shadows with a newfound peace and strength. Grief is good when it honestly expresses the hurts and hopes of the one who has suffered a loss. *Good* Grief!

Good Friday! This day is called *good* because it honestly expresses the heart of God in relationship to all humanity. "For God so loved the world, that he sent his only son...." Jesus, the Son of God, enfleshed the will of God to love men and women and children and the world itself to death — to love us to death, if that is what it took to bring us back into relationship with God.

This willingness to go all the way, one-sided, unconditioned, unsolicited, defines the nature of God's covenant with his creation.

God has covenanted never to abandon his world. The covenant of the rainbow in Noah's day was a heavenly sign that was sealed on earth in the blood of Jesus. Just as the American Indian would seal a promise and bond a relationship by mixing blood, so too God mixed the blood of Jesus into the history of the world to seal his promise given in the Garden and bond humanity to himself in an everlasting relationship of love. "I will remember their sins and their lawless deeds no more."

Good Friday is a day about relationship. God created us to live in relationship with him. "In the image of God he created them — male and female he created them." This is how the Bible opens the saga of creation and history. Adam and Eve, you and me, were created to live in relationship with God. As close as our breath, so close are we to be with our Creator, our cosmic lover and companion on our earthly trip through time and space.

But, the relationship has been broken. Adam and Eve disobediently stole some fruit from God's tree in the Garden; ever since, humanity has been robbed of a healthy relationship with God.

Augustine, a bishop of the early church, tells his story, which is really a reflection of our story. In his book *Confessions*, he admits to stealing fruit from a pear tree when he was seventeen years old. There was a pear tree near his family's vineyard. Now, Augustine was not poor, nor was he hungry. Yet, he stole pears from his neighbor's tree just for the joy of the theft. You might think, "Well, it was only a pear tree. I mean, we are not talking about adultery or murder or idolatry, or any of the 'big' sins."

Yes, we are! For there is no distinction in the eye of God. James writes in the New Testament, "Whoever keeps the whole law but fails in one point has become guilty of all of it." It is like being a little bit pregnant. You either are or you are not. So too with the law; we either keep it in its entirety, or we fail to keep it, no matter where we fall short. Paul reminds us about the truth of the matter: "All have sinned and fall short of the glory of God." The relationship with God has been broken. It does not matter if you stole a pear or killed your neighbor. Both acts come from the same disobedient heart. The result is the same — the relationship with God has been broken. It must be mended. Paul agonized, "Wretched man that I am; who will deliver me from this body of death?" We cannot accomplish it from our side of the relationship. God must do it from his side. That is exactly what God did on *Good* Friday.

Some people criticize Christianity as too morbid, focusing so much upon humanity's sinfulness. Danish theologian Soren Kierkegaard wrote, "Without the consciousness of sin, there is no Christianity." Of course, the truth hurts; but there is a purpose for our being so sensitive to this truth of our basic human sinfulness. It is like what Augustine wrote in his *Confessions*: "I reviewed my most wicked ways in the very bitterness of my remembrance, so that you may grow sweet unto me, O God." The purpose of remembering our sinfulness is to see the sweetness, the goodness of God.

Good Friday is not about *our* being good, worshiping God, and trying to get along with one another with the best of intentions, even as Paul admonishes us "to provoke one another to love and good deeds...." Good Friday is about *God* being good and forgiving us, even when we were no longer good to his only Son, whom we crucified. The words of Paul are like a two-edged sword cutting both ways: "God shows his love for us in that while we were yet sinners, Christ died for us."

This day, Good Friday, is the lens through which we see clearly just how much God loves us — not because we deserve it, but because we need it. What we deserve is death, since "the wages of sin is death." What we get instead is the death of Jesus, which covers the wage and sets us free to be children of God. The relationship is now restored, in the words of Paul who wrote, "All this is from God, who through Christ reconciled us to himself ... that is, in Christ God was reconciling the world to himself, not counting their trespasses against them...."

This is why we can come with confidence to the sanctuary of God's house. We are invited into a new and living way to be ourselves in the world. We are forgiven sinners, who can face the darkest Fridays of our lives with hope, because God is with us all the way all the time. He is faithful to his promises to be with us in the deepest valley, even unto the end of time. He is powerful to fulfill his promise. Neither sin nor death can stand in his way to do for us what he says he will do.

We can pray with Soren Kierkegaard, that melancholy Dane who prayed his way through cross-marked Fridays: "Lord, hold not our sins up against us, but hold us up against our sins; so that the thought of you, when it wakens in us and every time it wakens, may remind us not of how much we have sinned, but of how much you have forgiven us; not how we went astray, but how you saved us" (paraphrase).

Good Friday! It is a good day to die; it is a good day to live. Amen.

Easter Day   1 Corinthians 15:1-11

Witnesses

In a play about the crucifixion of Jesus, playwright John Masefield creates a conversation between Pilate's wife and one of the soldiers present at Golgotha. The soldier tells Pilate's wife that he does not think Jesus has remained dead and buried. When she asks where he might be, the soldier replies, "He is let loose in the world where no one can stop him."

Paul verifies this observation, as he recounts how many times Jesus appeared after the resurrection. No one was able to stop him, not even the guards at the tomb. Nothing was able to stop him, not even locked doors. Jesus appeared to Cephas and the disciples; then, to a large gathering of more than 500 believers; then, to James and all the other apostles. He even appeared to the prime persecutor and marauder of the Christian church, Saul, who later became known as Paul, the principle preacher and missionary of the faith. Let's not forget Mary, from whom Jesus had cast out seven demons, who gospel writers Mark and John report was the first to see the risen Jesus.

Jesus is let loose in the world. Witnesses, observe!

It is one thing to appear to believers who want to believe. It only took a gentle conversation in the morning mist of a garden to convince Mary that Jesus was "let loose."

It's another thing to appear to one's enemy and win him over. Saul encountered the risen Jesus in a blinding light on the road to Damascus. For three days he was without sight, fasting. It was not until a Christian stranger named Ananias came and healed him in the name of Jesus, that his heart was turned from hate to faith and he was baptized and ate.

There is a power in Christ's resurrection presence that changes people, empowering them to witness to his unconquerable, undying love.

Newspaper reports would have had a field day chasing after so many witnesses that Paul identifies — the band of apostles more than once, over 500 men and women at one time, and, of course, Paul himself, who had been one of the most vehement opponents to Jesus and his followers.

Let us move a few years away from these early events and meet another witness to the resurrection of Jesus, a man whose faith was an inspiration to many. His name was Marcellus, a Roman soldier. Marcellus had always wanted to be a legionnaire. When his opportunity came, he did his best to be the finest soldier possible. His superiors noticed his efforts and rewarded him with promotions. Marcellus was such a good soldier that he was promoted to the rank of centurion. What an honor! To receive this promotion, he needed to go through the ritual of bowing to an image of Caesar and proclaiming "Caesar is Lord."

This is where it got difficult. Marcellus was a Christian. He recognized that to go through this ritual would be to deny his faith that "Jesus is Lord." He refused to do so.

His superiors, sympathetic to his feelings, urged him repeatedly to do so. They wanted Marcellus as a trusted and worthy centurion in their ranks. They also reminded him that to refuse to bow before Caesar would invoke the death penalty. They did not want that to happen to one of their best soldiers. Marcellus bravely refused once again.

He was beheaded in front of his comrades. The ranking officer cajoled the troops, that if there were any other Christians they should step forward also. Amazingly, several did, knowing that a similar fate awaited them.

Marcellus had been actively witnessing about the crucified and risen Jesus at the same time he was soldiering. Many came to meet Jesus through Marcellus and became believers. Jesus is let loose and not even the discipline of the Roman Legion could restrain him.

Now, let us stride through history several centuries to another time and another place to meet another witness to the crucified and risen Jesus. The numbers simply multiply throughout the ages. When Jesus is let loose, neither time nor space can contain him.

The time is the thirteenth century. The place is Hungary. Elizabeth was the daughter of the king. A devout Christian from her childhood, Elizabeth had a generous spirit. Her arranged marriage to the son of the Landgrave of Thuringia secured her future in aristocratic society. However, her heart was with the poor and needy. When a severe famine occurred in the region, Elizabeth shared most of her personal fortune and grain with the poor.

Her compassion was not momentary. Seeing the needs of the sick in the community led her to establish two hospitals for their care. One of them was located at the foot of the Wartburg, where three hundred years later Martin Luther would be translating the witness accounts of the resurrection into German. Elizabeth herself would oftentimes be found in the hospitals, tending to the patients.

One time, when her husband Ludwig was away, Elizabeth had opportunity to provide care for a leper in her own home, even allowing him to sleep in her bed. When Ludwig returned, he was at first distraught at the sight, but then quickly recognized that his wife was serving the risen Christ, who had said, "Just as you did it to one of the least of these ... you do it to me."

There is power in the resurrection of Jesus to shape people's lives in marvelous ways. Because Jesus is let loose in the world, human lives can be let loose to rise above the worldly distinctions that separate us from one another. In Jesus we can be bonded in a love that crosses all barriers of status, wealth and health.

Now, let us journey to nineteenth century America for a brief visit to a graveyard for a simple witness to the resurrection of Jesus. Surrounding Andrew Jackson's Tennessee home is the family burial ground. One of the gravestones is for Annie Laurie Lawrence. The testimonial identifies her parents and the date of her death. A passage from the Psalms reads: "Precious in the sight of the Lord is the death of his saints." Then, from the closing of the Book of Revelation, "Come, Lord Jesus."

Yes, there is the reality of death. But, just as real is the reality of the resurrection of Jesus Christ. Because of this reality, there is hope even beyond the living of our days. When Christ comes again, as he has promised, he will raise us up also to share with him the victory won. With Cephas and James, Marcellus, Elizabeth and Annie, we will witness for eternity the power of the resurrection of Jesus over sin and death.

Paul assures us of this when he writes, "Therefore we have been buried with him by baptism into death, so that just as Christ was raised from the dead by the glory of the Father, so we too might walk in newness of life. For if we have been united with him in a death like his, we shall certainly be united with him in a resurrection like his."

It is true, then, that even twenty centuries later, we too are witnesses of the resurrection of Jesus. Baptism is the Christian's "portal of time" that brings us back to Jesus, which at the same time brings him forward into our lives today. Martin Luther, who shared the same Wartburg that Elizabeth of Thuringia grew up in, describes the Christian life as a daily return to one's baptism; for in baptism, the Christian has been united with the crucified and risen Lord Jesus Christ. To remember one's baptism is to journey once again to Golgotha and the empty tomb to witness the death and resurrection of Jesus. The gospel in which we stand proclaims this drama as the fulcrum of human history and the balance point for our personal lives.

What a joy it is for us to stand with so many witnesses from the first century and from all the centuries between then and now. Jesus is let loose in the world where no one can stop him. We are his witnesses, that others too may believe and find new life in his name. This life is characterized by the forgiveness of sin, deliverance from death and all evil, and the promise of life everlasting. Indeed, come, risen Lord Jesus. Amen.

Easter 2   1 John 1:1—2:2

Made — Lost
— And Found

The most personal question anyone can ask is *"Who am I?"* It is the fundamental question of our human existence.

Who is this person whose face reflects in the mirror every morning? Who is this person who laughs and cries, who works and plays, who eats and drinks and goes to the bathroom? Who is this person who hears and sees, smells, tastes and touches the world around?

In one of his delightful books, *Are You My Mother?*, P.D. Eastman portrays the agonizing search for an answer to this question. When a mother bird realizes that her egg is about to hatch, she flies off to get some food for it to eat when it is born. Before she can return, the egg hatches and the little bird emerges but does not know who or what it is. So it asks anything and everything it encounters if that thing is its mother; then, it will know who it is. The little bird asks a cow, a dog, a steam shovel, and a host of other things as it searches for its identity. The entire book portrays the steady searching of the little bird which does not stop and is not satisfied until it finds its mother.

Who am I? I am someone who is made by God! God was not absent when we came into the world. God was intimately present. "Then the Lord God formed man from the dust of the ground, and breathed into his nostrils the breath of life; and the man became a living being." I am someone whom God forms. God holds me in his hands and gives me shape. The great God who creates the universe and scatters the stars throughout the majestic heavens reaches down and caresses the earth so lovingly as to sculpture me as an original pattern. Then, in an act so selfless — for this great God does not want me to exist as an inanimate object for his pleasure only — this great God breathes into me his own breath and I become alive to experience the world for myself. What a gift! Human life is a gift! We are alive by the grace of God.

The story is told about a boy who was very clever and built a wooden boat for himself. This was the finest of boats. He spent hours and hours crafting it to his delight and making sure it was capable of floating. When it was ready, he sailed it in the water holes and rain-flooded ditches near his home. With a piece of string attached to the boat and with the power of his imagination, he could sail the mighty seas on deck as skipper.

One day he brought the boat to the river and played with it there. The river's current was swift and as the boat moved out into the middle, the string that kept the boat within its maker's reach broke and the boat was carried away downstream out of sight. The boy searched and searched, but it was almost like the boat was hiding on him or the river was playing tricks on him. He did not find the boat. It was lost.

Sometimes we feel like that boat: lost. We have times in our life when we feel detached, out of reach and out of touch with God, adrift on a fast current of life going places unknown. The Bible calls this lostness sin.

Sin is separating ourselves from God. Sin is breaking the line of obedience to God, just like Adam and Eve did in the Garden of Eden. Afterwards, they got "lost" in the bushes, hoping God would not find them, because they were conscious of their sin. Soren Kierkegaard, Danish theologian, writes, "Without the consciousness of sin, there is no Christianity." In our thoughts, words, and deeds we put ourselves into the swift currents of disobedience and become disconnected. The relationship with God is broken. We become lost to God.

Who am I? I am lost! Mark Twain, who plied the Mississippi River for many years, observes that our actions are what betray us, revealing the true character of our hearts. He graphically describes humanity with these pessimistic words: "Of all the animals, man is the only one that is cruel. He is the only one that inflicts pain for the pleasure of doing it ... He is the only animal that loves his neighbor as himself, and cuts his throat if his theology isn't straight." Martin Luther simply referred to "me, a lost and condemned person."

Let us return to the boy who lost his boat. He went searching and one day he passed a store. As he looked in through the window, he saw his boat in a pile of wood scraps in front of a stove. The store owner had scavenged the neighborhood for wood to keep him warm. The boy rushed in and told the store owner that the boat was his. He had made it; it got lost; but now he found it. "Just a minute, young man," the store owner said. "I worked hard finding all this wood for my stove and you just can't have it. How do I know you are telling the truth? You can pay me for it though. Then, I'll let you have it."

The boy ran out of the store and immediately went to work, for he loved his boat, his own creation. He soon had the money and returned to the store just as the store owner was about to use his boat in the next kindling for the fire. "Wait," he shouted. "I have what is needed." He handed his hard-earned money to the man by the fire, grabbed his boat and left. As he was walking down the street, holding on tightly to his little creation, he was overheard to say, "Now you are twice mine. First I made you; then I bought you."

God will not let his people remain lost. He searches for them on earth and through Jesus finds them. "We have an advocate with the Father, Jesus Christ the righteous," who paid the price for sin and saved us from the fires of judgment. The cradled Messiah, the boy King, the survivor of the wilderness temptations, the derelict on the cross, the resurrected Jesus has paid the price that saves us from the fires that would always burn our lives and separate us from God. He sheds his blood, "the atoning sacrifice for our sins," so that we can be found and doubly bound to God. "Now you are twice mine. First I made you. Then, I bought you."

Who am I? I am one who is found by God!

Made — Lost and Found! This is no lie. This is the story of life. This is the foundation for faith. With this message of God's love through Jesus, you are seized, clutched to the very heart of God, who wills not to let you go.

Who am I? I am made by God. I am lost, a sinner. I am found and doubly bound to be the delight of God, who now is my delight. Amen.

Easter 3   1 John 3:1-7

New Life From Old

Easter is in springtime for a reason. Springtime is that time of year when new life emerges from the old. Easter is that time of history when New Life emerged from the old.

You might well imagine the surprise of the first disciples when they discovered the empty tomb, and later when they had a close encounter with the risen Christ. Peter, in a journal-like comment, rehearses the events in his conversation with Cornelius and his family and friends: "We are witnesses to all that he did both in Judea and in Jerusalem. They put him to death by hanging him on a tree; but God raised him on the third day and allowed him to appear, not to all the people but to us who were chosen by God as witnesses, and who ate and drank with him after he rose from the dead."

We too have encountered the risen Christ through faith. We were not present at the empty tomb; we did not see the Lord as the disciples did, but yet we too believe. Jesus said to his disciples, "Have you believed because you have seen me? Blessed are those who have not seen and yet have come to believe."

Though we have not seen, we still have the privilege to eat and drink with our Lord. He has not left us without a sign of his resurrection, without a symbol of his eternal presence with his people. The close encounter continues. New life from old occurs as we receive Holy Communion, the family meal of the children of God, through which the crucified Jesus is truly present with us. Plain old bread is made into a witness of his body — crucified, yet risen. Common old wine is made into a witness of his blood — shed for you and for many for the forgiveness of sin. As we share in this sacred meal, we proclaim to the world that we are children of God now. God the Father has sent his Son for us, and by the power of the Holy Spirit we believe and are witnesses to the love of God for all people through Jesus Christ.

John's words describing his apostolic experience in his day are just as true for us today: "We have seen and do testify that the Father has sent his Son as the Savior of the world. God abides in those who confess that Jesus is the Son of God, and they abide in God. So we have known and believe the love that God has for us."

Just as the past is made present for believers through faith, so too is the future made present for believers through faith. New life from old *happened* through the historical events of Jesus 2,000 years ago, such that Paul wrote about the New Age dawning. New life from old *will also happen* in the resurrection unto life everlasting yet to come. *And* new life from old *is happening* today for believers through faith.

God does not give us merely a reflective faith that looks back and reminisces fondly. Nor does God give us only a far-flung hope into the future. God also gives us a present experience of new life from old. We *are* children of God, John writes. That is present tense reality. Paul expressed it this way, "You must consider yourselves dead to sin and alive to God in Christ Jesus."

Two caterpillars were crawling across the grass when they saw a butterfly flutter above them. One nudged the other and said, "You couldn't get me up in one of those things for a million dollars!"

Poor little caterpillars, can you not see what you may yet become? How much we are like these caterpillars! We become so familiar with what is, that we fail to see what God can make of us — new life from old.

The gospel challenges us with new life. Through faith, God gives us the opportunity to view life differently, from a loftier height, from a resurrection height. There are great possibilities of creative living yet ahead of us. God calls us to a winged existence of faith that leaves behind the old, cumbersome past, laden with sin and death.

Like the caterpillars who follow nature's course and become dead to their old form in their cocoon, we must awaken to the fact that our old life is not worth hanging on to. Paul writes, "No longer present your members to sin as instruments of wickedness, but present yourselves to God as those who have been brought from death to life, and present your members to God as instruments of righteousness."

Nicky Cruz came to this awareness. He was one of the most feared gang members in New York City, engaging in rumbles wearing a garbage can for protection and wielding a baseball bat for an instrument of destruction. When Nicky encountered the risen Lord Jesus, he received a new life through faith. He became an "instrument of righteousness" who was able to rise above the carnage of life on the street. He shared his newfound faith with others and led them to experience the power of new life in Jesus Christ. Just as the caterpillar has to be willing to die to the old self, so too the believer dies to an old life of sin.

Just as the butterfly replaces the caterpillar, so too there is a new life of faith that replaces the old life. What does that new life of faith look like?

There is an inherent danger in asking that question. It implies that one can *observe* the life of faith, as if it were an object to handle, put under the microscope, or display in a case. The life of faith is to be *lived*, not observed. God may indeed view it from the heavens, but as humans we can only perceive it by actually living it. Entomologists and curious children observe butterflies. But, the butterfly itself is totally involved in the art of flying and finding nectar daily to sustain its new life beyond the cocoon.

This danger acknowledged, let us dare to ask the question about the appearance of the new life. One of the Christian classics in literature is the book by Thomas a Kempis, *The Imitation of Christ*, considered by some "the most perfect flower of medieval Christianity." The essential message of this work is that the Christian life is to be like Christ, following in his footsteps. Martin Luther was fond of saying that we are to be "little Christs" to our neighbors.

What would such a life look like? There are two things that immediately come to mind that can apply to every Christian life. First, the new life is characterized by *forgiveness*. Jesus taught us to pray, "And forgive us our debts, as we also have forgiven our debtors." In one of the parables of the kingdom, he reminded us that we are to forgive one another, just as God has forgiven us. When Peter asks him how many times a person should forgive, "As many as seven times?" Jesus responds with an exaggerated sense of unlimited forgiveness, "Seventy times seven."

Forgiveness is the diamond in the treasure of Christian virtues. It is old hat to hold grudges and be bitter toward others because of some action in the past. It is powerfully new and refreshing for the relationship when a person is able to forgive. Let go and let God rebuild the relationship that had been lost.

The windmills of Holland were built to reclaim land lost to the ocean, so that it can be fertile for growth. Forgiveness is the windmill of Christian faith, reclaiming lost land in relationships, so that they can grow and flourish once again.

To imitate Christ means to be willing to forgive. This willingness and this ability to forgive is a resurrection reality for those who believe in Christ.

Forgetting not is the old life; *forgiving now* is the new life.

Second, the new life is characterized by *service*. On Thursday evening before his crucifixion, Jesus washed the disciples' feet. He said, "If I, your Lord and Teacher, have washed your feet, you also ought to wash one another's feet. For I have set you an example, that you also should do as I have done to you." The new life in Christ imitates Christ, and that means a life of service.

For centuries the servant's role has been considered one of lowly origin. The servant's quarters were distinct from the main house; the servant's entrance was around the side or in back, not at the main gate into the estate. In God's brave new world, it is the servant who is elevated to the status of the right hand of God. The first shall be last and the last shall be first. Jesus responded to the issue of greatness in this way: "Whoever wishes to be great among you must be your servant ... just as the Son of Man came not to be served but to serve, and to give his life a ransom for many."

Selfishness is the old life; *service* is the new life.

There was once a widow who visited the cemetery weekly. Tears were shed and bitter words expressed, as she reminded her husband of how he was so careless with his diet and ate himself into an early grave.

One day the pastor happened to walk by and noticed her standing by the headstone. He approached just in time to hear her describe the kind of meals she tried to fix for him, but which he refused to eat, preferring to snack on high fat, high salt foods instead.

"Sounds like you are still mad at George," the pastor said quietly.

"Sure am," the woman responded. "Why does he keep doing this to me? I can still see him late at night at the kitchen table, eating a greasy sandwich."

"I don't see where he is doing anything to you anymore, Mary," the pastor observed. "You are the one who won't change the channel in your mind."

"How can I? That's exactly what he would do."

"Yes, but you could forgive him for such decisions he made and then get on with your life. Right now, your anger is burying you with him."

Those words startled Mary into seeing how she was holding on to her anger at her husband, not forgiving him. "Am I still nagging my husband?" she thought to herself. She had been experiencing a certain smugness in his inability to answer her now.

"O, God in heaven," she sighed, "how could I be so mean?"

The pastor did not see Mary in the cemetery much anymore. The next time he did see her was at the community meal site for senior citizens, cooking over a hot stove, providing nutritious dinners for those who are on meager incomes or do not eat well alone.

God does not cotton much to graveyard people. The tomb is empty and God is with his people who are on the move, striving to live. God is a God of action, constantly bringing new life from old.

This new life from old happened dramatically, historically once for all in the life, death, and resurrection of Jesus Christ. It will certainly happen at the end of time, when Christ comes again. In the meantime, it is happening daily, as the breath of God gives flight to those who spread their wings of faith and learn how to imitate Christ in forgiveness and service. Amen.

Easter 4 1 John 3:16-24

Love In Action

One of the enduring images of both the Old Testament and New Testament scriptures is that of the good shepherd. The Psalmist, the prophet Ezekiel, and Jesus himself used this human picture to convey a divine reality. The picture is that of the shepherd who cares well for his sheep, even to the point of laying down his life for the sheep; the divine reality is that the Son of God cares for us so much that he was willing to lay down his life for us. This love creates new life in us, so that we desire to be loving to those around us.

The good shepherd is the one who will lead the sheep. He will go before the sheep to test the way. The sheep will confidently follow, because they see that the shepherd has gone before them, through the narrow passages and over the danger-laden pathways. The writer to the Hebrews says that Jesus was tempted in every way just like we are; yet he is without sin, so that he can indeed help those who are so tempted. Like sheep, as we follow Jesus, he can lead the way for us through the danger zones.

The good shepherd is the one who will care for the sheep when they gather in the corral after a day of grazing. They eat the grass down to the nub, scratching their sensitive noses on the rocks and the earth. The good shepherd waits by the door of the corral and applies a soothing salve on their noses to heal the bruises for tomorrow's pasture. The Gospel of Matthew reports Jesus' salving words, "Come to me, all who labor and are heavy laden, and I will give you rest." This he did for the lepers, the blind, the lame, the possessed, the grieving and the dead.

The good shepherd is the one who will stand between the sheep and any danger. When the wolf attacks the fold, the shepherd, the one who is good, will challenge the intruder. To get to the sheep, the wolf has to get by the good shepherd first. The wolf may be hungry, but will he risk his life for a meal? The good shepherd will risk his life for the sake of the sheep. Here is where Jesus demonstrates his love for us in the greatest way possible. Jesus puts his life on the battle line between us and our spiritual enemies: sin and death. They will seek to defeat and capture us, separating us from God. To the victor belongs the spoils. It is a fight to the finish. Jesus sacrifices himself to the enemy in order to save us. Evil gloats for a weekend, but God turns the tide of battle on the third day. On Easter morning Jesus bursts from the tomb and proclaims that he himself is the victor. "I am the resurrection and the life. Those who believe in me, even though they die, will live, and everyone who lives and believes in me will never die."

It is in the spirit of this kind of divine love that John in his pastoral letter encourages believers to be loving. "We know love by this, that he laid down his life for us — and we ought to lay down our lives for one another." In times of persecution, this makes literal sense, when believers may be called upon to lose their lives in order to protect others from being exposed to authorities who seek their harm; for example, Christians were called upon to do just this during World War II when Nazis hunted Jews.

However, John goes on to describe how this kind of love is also expressed when we respond to the needs of those around us with Christ-like love. The Good Shepherd calls for his sheep to be good.

Consider Alice. She knew the Good Shepherd. The Good Shepherd called her to be a good sheep. Alice had a son whom she loved deeply. But a tragic death snatched him away in his youth from her mothering arms. Alice knew the Good Shepherd. He came to her in the depth of her broken heart. She resolved to remember her precious son in a way that would reach out to help other youth. Every year, since his death, she provides a campership for any youth who wants to go to Bible camp but who has financial difficulties getting there. Alice is a good sheep, who loves, "not in word or speech, but in truth and action."

Consider Lynn. Faithfully she would go to the nursing home to see her mother, who had aged not so gracefully. Alzheimer's clouded her mind and she did not even recognize her own daughter. But Lynn knew the Good Shepherd and how the Good Shepherd takes care of the sheep. Lynn determined to be the hands and voice of the Good Shepherd for her mother. Every visit she would carefully brush her mother's hair, snow white now and thinning, but still long and soft. It broke her heart to hear in weak response, "And who are you, dear?" Sometimes as she combed her hair, she would sing for her mom between the tears, sing songs that she learned on her mother's knee years ago. "That's lovely, dear. God bless you. Your name again?" Lynn is a good sheep, who loves "not in word or speech, but in truth and action."

Toyohiko Kagawa, a Japanese man, also knew the Good Shepherd. He became a Christian as a teenager. It cost him dearly to love the Lord, because his family disinherited him. They did not want a Christian in their traditional Japanese family. Yet, Kagawa persevered in his newfound faith. After years of study in Tokyo, he returned to his hometown of Kobe. He was concerned for the poor of Kobe, so he lived in a six-foot by six-foot hut in one of the worst slums in the world. He worked to establish the first labor union in Japan among shipyard workers. He also founded the Farmer's Union. His efforts did not always meet with the approval of the authorities. Twice he was arrested because of his efforts on behalf of the working people. His faith in the Good Shepherd led him to see the face of God in the faces of the poor and oppressed people of Japan. He established credit unions, schools, hospitals, and churches throughout Japan on their behalf.

In one of his writings, Kagawa expressed this: "My real experience of religion came when I entered the Kobe slums. Everything in the slums was ugly: the people, the houses, the clothes, the streets — everything was ugly and full of disease. If I had not carried God beside me, I should not have been able to stay. But because I believed in God ... I had a different view of life ... My job was to help these people ... A gambler, dying, said to me that he was going back to his Heavenly Father. Then for the first time, like a flash, I was convinced that any person, even the most depraved, is able to grasp the [hand of the Good Shepherd]."[1]

Toyohiko Kagawa — this sheep became a ram with strong horns to butt against the wrongs of the world. He offered his wool and mutton, his life's breath and work, to the Good Shepherd; or as John expresses it, "... to obey his commandments and do what pleases him ... and this is his commandment, that we should believe in the name of his Son Jesus Christ and love one another...."

John writes a letter of encouragement to all of us today in light of the resurrection of our Lord Jesus Christ: "Little children, let us love, not in word or speech, but in truth and action." Alice, Lynn, and Kagawa did so. This is how the Lord abides in us today. Amen.

---

1. Toyohiko Kagawa, *Love: The Law Of Life* (St. Paul, Minn.: Macalester Park Publishing Co., 1951), pp. 13-14. Used by permission.

Easter 5   1 John 4:7-21

Love And Friendship

A boy was asked about his family, when he enrolled for church school. The teacher responded with a quizzical, "Oh," after the boy revealed that he had no brothers or sisters. To which the youngster piped, "But I've got friends!"

It is so good to have friends. But, what is a friend? Satirist Ambrose Bierce defines friendship as a ship big enough to carry two in fair weather, but only one in foul. This is a rather negative portrayal compared to an Arabian explanation that characterizes a friend as "one to whom one may pour out all the contents of one's heart, chaff and grain together, knowing that the gentlest of hands will take it and sift it, keep what is worth keeping, and with the breath of kindness blow the rest away."

In the Gospel of John, Jesus talks about love and friendship in the same breath. He calls his disciples friends, immediately after describing the greatest love as one person willingly laying down his or her life for a friend. True friendship is most clearly seen in this kind of love. It is a friendship that essentially gives of itself to another.

To say that an individual is *my friend* is to recognize something special that an individual has done for you. It is not that you did something nice for that person which qualifies that one as your friend. Rather, it is how the individual treats you that determines one's friendship. Friendship is essentially founded upon what someone else does *for you*. The same is true with love.

In his pastoral letter, John expresses this so well. "God's love was revealed among us in this way: God sent his only Son into the world so that we might live through him. In this is love, not that we loved God but that he loved us and sent his Son to be the atoning sacrifice for our sins."

When Jesus discusses friendship with his disciples in the Gospel of John, he speaks about it in terms of laying down his life, offering up his life. The sign of a true friend is the willingness to give up one's life for the sake of the one befriended. Against the Old Testament background of "sacrifice for sin," Jesus is willing to accept the responsibility to become the sacrifice for sin for all, so that God's love can be extended to all. Jesus becomes our friend by paying the price for our sin. He does *for us* that which the law requires, namely the shedding of our blood. Capital punishment is the verdict rendered by God for our rebellion. We are to pay the price! Except that our friend, Jesus, intervenes and sacrifices himself on our behalf.

What a friend we have in Jesus, as the familiar hymn reminds us. Jesus chose us to befriend. We did not choose him to be our friend. As he himself said, "You did not choose me but I chose you." The nature of friendship is that it chooses who shall benefit from the relationship. Friendship can be given as well as taken away, unlike the givenness of kinship.

The following is a true story that occurred during the internment of Christian missionaries in a Japanese prison camp in the Philippines during World War II. It was the rule of the camp that anyone caught trying to escape would be put to death. One day a little-noticed, "unimportant" prisoner broke out of the compound for freedom, but was caught. He was a small, dirty, hairy individual, whose life seemed to have no great significance to the Japanese or to the imprisoned Americans. The guards placed the man in the middle of the yard and assembled all the other prisoners to watch his execution.

It was also a rule of the camp that any prisoner breaking rank during assembly would be executed at once. The small, dirty, hairy man was staked to the ground. The guards began to whip him, the intention being to whip him to death. Suddenly, the doctor — of all people, the doctor! — broke rank. The doctor was the one camp prisoner who was indispensable. It was his knowledge and care that helped keep the other prisoners alive in the face of malnutrition, dysentery, malaria, and fatigue. But, the doctor broke rank, aware of the consequences, and threw himself over the body of that man, staked out for death. He put his own precious body between the whip and the small, dirty, hairy back of the doomed man. The guards were so impressed with such an act of self-sacrificing bravery that they let both men live.

The doctor proved to be more than a fair-weather friend to the man.

Friendship is made manifest when the friend acts in some special way *for you*. Love is made manifest when the friend acts in some special way *for you*.

"No one has greater love than this, to lay down one's life for one's friends." Jesus said this; Jesus did this!

The Law of God condemns us as sinners and sentences us to death. Jesus puts himself between the whip of the Law and our backs. He takes the blows himself. The prophet Isaiah pictures it this way:

> *He was wounded for our transgressions,*
> *crushed for our iniquities;*
> *upon him was the punishment that made us whole,*
> *and by his bruises we are healed.*

Jesus is no fair-weather friend! He rides out the storm with us and for us, not just to the edge of doom, but even over the edge of doom.

A contemporary hymn by James S. Tallman puts it this way:

> *A friend is a friend who will come to his friends,*
> *Whenever in trouble he sees us.*
> *A friend is a friend who will give to his friends,*
> *From every worry relieves us.*

Many will come and claim to be friends,
But we can be sure that it's true in the end
That a friend is a friend who will die for his friends.
We have a friend in Jesus![1]

Jesus, who hung on the scaffold of judgment for us, who laid down his life for us, is the same Jesus who was raised from the dead by the power of God. He lives today! He calls us to follow him as friends. He has befriended us and invites us to be friends to one another in his name. In other words, what Jesus gives to us, he calls out of us to give in turn to one another, as the following story illustrates.

Little did Arleen know how their life would be challenged and changed by the knock on the door that early Friday morning. The officers had a warrant for Edgar. Apparently he had been rotating company funds illegally, borrowing money from certain policies to make investments for clients. If he had more time, he would have been able to put all the monies back in place, so that nobody would have lost anything. But, an accountant discovered the irregularities and blew the whistle. Edgar had no defense for his guilt. For the next five years he resided at the state penitentiary. He was relieved of his responsibilities at work. His reputation was lost. His family was devastated. Arleen had a big decision. Hurt and angered by the turn of events, she could have left her husband of 27 years. He had failed her trust in him, after all.

"Are you going to leave me?" Edgar asked plaintively from behind the glass window that separated them in the visitors' room.

"What do you expect me to do?" she responded with anger.

"I've really blown it, Arleen. I am so sorry. I didn't think I was doing anything wrong at the time. But now, I see how many lives I've messed up. I am so sorry." Edgar could hardly look at her as he spoke.

"You have hurt the family, Edgar," Arleen said sternly. "I would like to walk away from here and not look back ... and not remember any of this ... But I can't." Arleen spoke in a softer tone now.

"What are you saying, Arleen?" Edgar asked with an edge of hope in his voice.

"I'm saying that if my marriage vows mean anything to me, I will stay with you through this. If my faith means anything to me, I will stay with you through this. If God's promises are true, God will stay with us through this. That's what I'm saying, Edgar. It's not easy to say right now, but I know it is the right thing to say — to believe." Arleen put her hand against the window for a moment and then removed it to wipe away her tears.

"Thank you, Arleen. I know this is not easy for you. I've told you before how much your affection has meant to me over the years, but it is only now that I am beginning to see the depth of your heart. I don't deserve you." Edgar was choking back the lump of grief gathering in his throat.

"No, perhaps you don't. But I'm here and I won't leave you, Edgar." Her hand returned to the glass. Edgar reached for it with his. Five years of glass now separated them. Pressing hard against its smooth surface, Edgar could already feel her gentle hand penetrate the barrier, sifting the grain and the chaff of his life, keeping what is worth keeping and giving him hope.

Arleen's realistic and dedicated love for Edgar embody Shakespeare's words when he writes:

> ... *Love is not love*
> *Which alters when it alteration finds...*
> *O, no! it is an ever-fixed mark,*
> *That looks on tempests and is never shaken;*
> ... *Love alters not with his brief hours and weeks,*
> *But bears it out even to the edge of doom.*

God's love for us did not alter when sin was found in our hearts. God remained steadfast to the covenant of love that infused God's creation from the beginning. This is the kind of love we are to emulate in our relations with one another. Arleen struggled well with this challenge. As John writes, "Beloved, since God loved us so much, we also ought to love one another."

In the power of the resurrection life, Christians are inspired to model every relationship after the love and friendship offered for us, given to us, and worked through us by the Lord Jesus Christ, our loving friend in deed and indeed. Amen.

---

1. Reprinted from "*Church Songs* #1: A Friend Is A Friend," music and lyrics by James S. Tallman, copyright © 1995 James S. Tallman. Used by permission of James S. Tallman.

Easter 6   1 John 5:1-6

The Victory
Of Faith

Planes drop out of the sky, killing all passengers. Mini-dictators initiate programs of genocide against neighbors. Forces of nature storm across the landscape, leaving devastation in their path. Bizarre individual behavior leaves heads shaking, "How can anyone do such things?" Accidents at home and on the highway steal loved ones away.

All this gives credence to the sardonic line of a poem, which begins, "It's a wonderful world to be born into, if you don't mind a touch of hell now and then."

How do we respond to "a touch of hell now and then"?

Do we go on a binge of moralism, chiding the sinfulness of a wicked world? Do we start off on a tirade against the irresponsible decisions people make? Over cups of coffee, do we chastise parents for ineffectiveness in exercising control and influence in shaping their children's lives? Alone and in front of a mirror, do we berate ourselves over the personal failures in our own lives?

All of us respond to the evil and tragedies in the world by engaging in moralism, judgmentalism, pointing fingers at others, and devaluing ourselves, especially when the evil and tragedy touches our lives. To do these things, however, is like tying a millstone around the neck with the expectation of still swimming in ten feet of water. There is no good news here; only the weight of a law that there will certainly be more of the same day after day. All of our moralism, judgmentalism, pointing of fingers, and breaking our own mirrors will not change this.

The root issue at stake in all of these things is whether or not we can still believe in a good and gracious God. Please, do not misunderstand at this point. The issue is not whether God *is* good and gracious. God is! And God is good! And God is love! God *is* good and gracious. The psalmist, in reflecting upon the activity of God in history on behalf of his people, creating them as a nation and freeing them from bondage in Egypt, writes, "He has done marvelous things."

The root issue is whether we can **believe** in a good and gracious God, whether we can **trust** that God's redemptive purposes for the world and the lives of all in the world will finally triumph. Again, the psalmist is convinced, "His right hand and his holy arm have gotten him victory." Can we assent to this? Can we experience the victory of faith that the Bible talks about? How?

We are encouraged by the psalmist to "sing to the Lord a new song." Can we "break forth into joyous song and sing praises," with all that is happening around us? Can we find the courage of faith to believe in a good and gracious God despite being touched by hell "now and then"?

Recall the experience of God's people in the wilderness after being freed from under the oppressive hand of the Pharaoh. Their memory was short. They began to complain against God because the way was difficult. At least in Egypt they had food to eat and they knew where they were. In the wilderness, although they were free, they had to go from day to day for each meal and they really did not know where they were. This was unchartered wilderness where they had never been before. So, they murmured against the Lord.

Scripture reminds us over and over again that "the Lord is gracious and full of compassion, slow to anger and of great kindness." This was demonstrated in the wilderness. In their discomfort, the people argued, "God, why are you doing this to us? Make it a little easier. Give us a break!" Although the people murmured against the Lord, God did not send them back to Egypt;

nor did he obliterate them in a sandstorm. He had freed them; he would not go back on his word. He did, however, discipline them. There was an infestation of snakes in the camp of God's people. Many were bitten; many died. When they realized their foolishness, they prayed to God for help. God responded by having Moses set up a bronze snake in the midst of the people. Whenever they looked to the bronze snake, even though they were bitten, they would live and not die. It was their faith in God, their willingness to trust in the goodness of God even in the midst of terrible times, that gave them life. They had been birthed by God into freedom; as they trusted God with their lives, especially in the midst of the wilderness, they experienced "the victory that conquers the world."

Jesus referred to this wilderness event when Nicodemus, a Pharisee and leader of the Jews, came to him one night. Nicodemus wanted to understand Jesus more fully. He acknowledged that Jesus came from God; "for no one can do these signs that you do apart from the presence of God," he said. Then, he asked Jesus how he himself could be born of God. Jesus responded with this comparison: "Just as Moses lifted up the serpent in the wilderness, so must the Son of Man be lifted up, that whoever believes in him may have eternal life. For God so loved the world that he gave his only Son, so that everyone who believes in him may not perish but may have eternal life."

Yes, because the children of God did not believe in the goodness of God, there was an infestation of snakes among the people. There was discipline in the desert. Yet, the Lord still held his people in the hollow of his hand and did not deliver them entirely over to the powers of destruction. The Lord held true to his promises and eventually led his people across the Jordan and past the crumbling walls of Jericho and through the Philistine encampment, where not even Goliath was able to stop God's purposes for his people.

What a God in whom to believe! What a God in whom to trust! From the psalmist the refrain rises, "All the ends of the earth have seen the victory of our God."

The miracles of Jesus embody the presence and power of God to lift up those who have been stricken. Lepers were cleansed, the crippled were enabled to walk, the sick were healed, and the blind were restored to sight. Even the dead were raised. People who had been bowed down by life were lifted up by the love of God through Jesus.

Jesus is God's ensign to the world, just as the bronze snake was an ensign to the people in the wilderness. Jesus was lifted up on the scaffold of evil, bearing the brunt of its force in his person, accepting the pain of the world that is touched by hell now and then. Whoever looks to him, just like the people in the wilderness looked to the bronze snake, will be saved. This salvation is not some fantastic exemption from the ravages of evil. Evil will still have its *day*. The victory of faith is that God will finally have his *way*.

Think about it! The people who were cured by Jesus certainly experienced other aches and pains of daily life, just like we do. Lazarus, though raised from the dead, did indeed die again and was laid to rest to wait for the final resurrection. Life is still tough, even for the people of God. Paul had his thorn in the side; could it have been epilepsy? Peter was hung upside-down in martyrdom. The great reformer Martin Luther had bouts with depression. His namesake, Martin Luther King, Jr., was assassinated. They all still confirmed that God is good and gracious. The question for us is this: Do we have the courage of faith to trust in our good and gracious God even in the darkness of the night? If we do, our faith will give us the victory of light in the night.

In rejection and death, Jesus entrusted himself to the care of God, his Heavenly Father. "Father, into your hands I commit my spirit." This was done on the cross against all odds.

In the crucible of our human experiences, we can fall into thinking that something could actually separate us from the love of God. Faith overcomes this. Faith conquers this worldly temptation. The believer trusts that in Jesus God has done all that is truly necessary to overcome the darkness of the world with the light of his love.

A few years ago there was a national gathering of Christian youth in Dallas, Texas. A bus driver, who escorted a group of teenagers from Wisconsin, was tragically shot in the motel parking lot in a senseless act of violence. His daughter, Becky, wrote a letter to the Christian youth from other areas who responded to the family grief with prayers, letters of encouragement and memorial gifts of love. Here is a portion of her response. It reflects the victory of faith that can conquer the worst that the world can hurl at us.

Dear Christian friends,

Thank you so much for your prayers, letters, and money, which will be put towards a scholarship for students attending our local Christian high school.

When I first heard that my dad had been murdered, I believed that the world was a horrible place that had no good in it, but then when so many people sent cards, or visited, or called, I realized how wrong my thinking was. No matter how bad the day may seem, God always does something to make it better. Although I want to ask "Why him?" I realize that God has a plan and everything will work out. I could not imagine going through this without my faith or without Christ to lean on. He has comforted me in so many ways.

My family and I are trying to put our lives back together again. It's hard, but we have each other to lean on ... It gets a little easier with each day.

Your letter and gift, because it was from Christian people my age, really meant a lot. Thanks so much.

Sincerely,
Becky.[1]

Amen, Becky! You have experienced the victory of faith. Since this event, Becky has pursued a career that engages her in the rehabilation of criminals. Faith enables us to conquer the world. May we all share such a faith and know the victory of our Lord and Savior, Jesus Christ. Amen.

---

1. Used with permission..

Ascension Day   Ephesians 1:15-23

The Name Of Names

Mark — warlike
Shirley — bright meadow
Jennifer — fair lady
Jeffrey — God's peace
Jesus — God saves

What's in a name? Ever since God gave Adam the privilege of naming all the creatures, humankind has had a fascination with names. Names are important. Parents take great care when they select a name for their baby. They know the name will be with this new person for a lifetime and will identify him or her to other people.

We look at the panorama of history and give different names to the ages: Ice Age, Stone Age, Bronze Age, Dark Ages, Middle Ages, Modern Age, Post-Modern Age. The names help us distinguish periods of time and cultural growth or decline. The names, carefully chosen, give us a sense of where we fit in, regarding the development of civilization.

We characterize events with names, so that we can understand their nature and remember what they were like: the Depression, the Holocaust, the Civil Rights Movement, the Space Race.

What's in a name? An awful lot! Names help us have a handle on reality. Names help us identify, understand, and remember.

The writer to the Ephesian Christians says that the name of Jesus the Christ is "above every name that is named, not only in this age but also in the age to come." Jesus is Lord! There is no one, no power, no experience that can overshadow, or outdistance, or overcome what Jesus has done for you and for all. Jesus is raised from the dead and seated at the right hand of God. He is the head over all things. His name is above every other named reality. The name of Jesus means "God saves."

For Christians all things find their meaning, their context, their purpose, their value as they relate to Jesus. Paul advised his fellow Christians to live in such a way that whatever they said or did would be done in the name of Jesus.

What's in a name? Everything! For Christians the name of Jesus *identifies* the center of all meaning: the love of God through Jesus. For Christians the name of Jesus helps us *understand* how God expresses his love for us: through this crucified and risen one. For Christians the name of Jesus helps us *remember* that God is still with us in all his power to save. He said, "Remember, I am with you always, to the end of the age." We live, naming the name of names.

Knowing his name gives us a power in life! If I'm in a dark room, I have a distinct advantage if I know where the light switch is, if I can call forth the light. The gospel writer John names Jesus as the light of the world. "The light shines in the darkness, and the darkness did not overcome it."

As Christians we can name the light that dispels the fearsome shadows and dark corners of our human existence: Jesus, that name of names.

Let us lift up his name and carry it boldly into our world. Life is to be lived fully in the name of Jesus through what we say and through what we do; for, through Jesus, God saves.

In the ascension story in scripture, we read that Jesus was "lifted up," and "was carried up into heaven." The suffering, crucified and buried Jesus rose from the dead and ascended to heaven, victorious over the evil dark that would engulf this world. Jesus rules! This is what is meant by the scriptures when Jesus is portrayed sitting at the right hand of the Father. We acknowledge his lordship when we confess in the Apostles' Creed that "he ascended into heaven and is seated at the right hand of the Father." We name Jesus as the Lord of life in whose power we dare to face the challenges of each day.

We name his name and we are named by his name. Among the artists of Japan it was common for the master artist to give a new name to an exceptional student, forming this name by using a portion of his own name in the new name for the student. Genyemon Ando received the name Hiroshige from his master instructor Toyohiro. Hiroshige's woodblock prints are world-famous, influencing other great artists, like French impressionist Claude Monet. Anyone familiar with Hiroshige's work would, by his name, be reminded of his master, Toyohiro, a part of whose name he bore.

Christians bear the name of Jesus, as we are called by his name: Christ's ones. We are identified with him. We are one body with him, himself as the head. As part of him, we share in his victory, his power, his rule. He is ascended and he lifts up those who call upon his name. As the Psalmist expresses it, "Cast your burden on the Lord, and he will sustain you."

A curious Sunday School student asked one morning in class, "If Jesus is seated at the right hand of the Father, who is seated on the left?" The answer to that straightforward question is "We are!" We have been called to share in the immeasurable greatness of his power over sin, death and all evil. As the writer to the Ephesians states, "You may know what is the hope to which he has called you, what are the riches of his glorious inheritance among the saints, and what is the immeasurable greatness of his power for us who believe, according to the working of his great power."

Richard was recently afflicted with a prolonged and painful illness shortly after the death of his wife of 25 years. When asked how he was bearing up under the grief and disappointments, he replied, "It sure ain't easy. There are times when it is hard to get out of bed in the morning to start the day. But, my Lord is with me and he will give me the strength I need for each day. I simply have to trust in him and get on with it." In the midst of adversity, Richard was drawing on his inheritance, which empowered him to deal with his situation.

Charles Dickens begins his celebrated *A Tale of Two Cities* with this sentence: "It was the best of times; it was the worst of times." There will always be those "worst of times" as we face hardships, unemployment, war, poverty, injustice, hunger, sin and guilt, heartache, disappointments, setbacks, and death. But for Christians it is at the same time "the best of times," as we name the name of Jesus and by the power of his love are lifted up with courage and hope, strength and patience, forgiveness and kindness to live in the light of God's new day. The night has no power to overcome us, for all things have been put under Jesus' feet, like a footrest for the emperor who sits on the throne.

Live each day with the knowledge that Jesus is ascended. Jesus rules. His name is above all names. By his name you are called. Through his name you are saved. In his name you are blessed. Do not be afraid. Take heart. Be of good cheer. Pray boldly and live more boldly still. Amen.

Easter 7 1 John 5:9-13

Life In His Name

In 1922, a marvelous treasure was unearthed in the Valley of the Kings in Egypt. The tomb of King Tut, a nineteen-year-old pharaoh, was discovered. He lived 1,300 years before Jesus. One of the valued artifacts that was brought out of this ancient tomb was the figure of "The King upon a Leopard." The leopard was black, the shade of death. The pharaoh was clothed in bright, gilded color, riding regally upon the leopard's back. This figure of "The King upon a Leopard" symbolized the belief that King Tut would traverse the darkness of death, emerging into the brightness of a new day. Oil lamps and candles filled the tomb, which was dark as death. These lamps and candles would provide a light for King Tut to see his way through the darkness. There were other treasures also surrounding the mummified remains of the Egyptian monarch, treasures which would assist him on his journey. Of course, King Tut remains mummified, dead as darkness, and his candles are still waiting to be lit.

What a contrast to the simplicity of Jesus' tomb, in which only the folded grave clothes were found. Jesus, of course, was not there. He had risen. The darkness did not hold him captive until some archaeologist unearthed him. God the Father unearthed Jesus on the third day, raising him to glory because of his obedience unto death, even death on the cross. The scripture had been fulfilled where it was written, "Arise, shine; for your light has come, and the glory of the Lord has risen upon you."

The ancient Egyptians longed for light in the darkness, life after death. Christ Jesus *is* the light in the darkness and the darkness has not overcome him. Christ Jesus *is* the life after death and death is swallowed up in victory. We can parade before the many treasures of King Tut's tomb and look upon his mummified remains. But, before Jesus Christ we can only bow down and worship him, for **he** is the living one, alive forever — in his person, the very treasure of his empty tomb.

It is the Easter season of the church year. It is the season to rejoice in the light that has come and shined in the darkness of our world. Sin and death no longer have the upper hand in our lives. We do sin, yes; we will die, yes. But, Christ has conquered sin and death through his death and resurrection. We are now free to live in the power of that victory — to live over against our own sins, to live over against our own death.

The fifty days after Easter, which make up the Easter season of the church year, are designed to help us rejoice in the resurrection. If Lent focuses our attention *to* the cross of Christ, Easter focuses our attention *from* his empty tomb. Jesus died, yes; but, he is risen. Yes, indeed! "Do not be afraid," Jesus says. "I am the first and the last ... I was dead, and see, I am alive forever and ever."

What difference does that make? That is a good question with which to come to terms personally. What difference does the resurrection of Jesus Christ make in your life today?

You can have joy in your life. That is the first difference the resurrection of Jesus Christ can make in your life today.

When Jesus says, "Father, forgive them; for they do not know what they are doing," you can rest assured that those sins are indeed forgiven. Jesus died on the cross to pay for your sins. His resurrection is God's approval that he paid the price in full.

The resurrection confirms that when Jesus said, "It is finished," he was right. It is finished. He had accomplished all that he was sent to do — to lay down his life for the world. Paul writes, "In Christ God was reconciling the world to himself." When Jesus says, "It is finished," he means that the reconciliation is complete.

You and I, who had been enemies with God, are now made friends with God through Jesus Christ. It is finished. The battle is over. God has won. You and I are captured by the love of God and made friends with God, because God wants us to be his own.

This brings joy into life. Our sins are forgiven by the grace of God. Our death is overcome and will not separate us from the love of God. That is good news that puts bounce into every step and a smile on every face for those who hear it and believe it. In the words of Paul, "Rejoice in the Lord always; again I will say, Rejoice." You can have joy in your life because of the resurrection of Jesus Christ.

You can have meaning in your life. That is a second difference the resurrection of Jesus Christ can make in your life today. Does it really matter that you are alive?

When we become depressed, we think not. When we let the dark news of our world fill our minds and hearts, we think not. When we look to our own death and see only our mummified remains, we think not. BUT, the news of the day is that Jesus is risen! So, YES! It really does matter that you are alive. For Jesus came to seek and to save YOU. You are precious in his sight. Like the children's song expresses it, "Red and yellow, black and white, all are precious in his sight...."

There is meaning in your life because God created you and God does not make junk! There is meaning in your life because Christ died for you. He calls you friend; and greater love than this has no one, that he lay down his life for his friend.

So often one can hear it said by people who have had a scrape with death, "There must be a reason for me to still be here." Yes, indeed! There is a reason for all of us to be here. We have a life to live! God gave us that life. God means for us to live it. The meaning for life is to be and to become, to live and to grow. Death does not have the final word. The God of Life does! Death cannot strip away the meaning of your life, as if at best you are just a cipher in the snow. No! Jesus is risen and he is the Lord of Life. Your life means the world to God, as the psalmist says, "Guard me as the apple of the eye." Your life is graciously held in the palm of God's victorious right hand, and he will not let go of you.

You can have something to say with your life. That is the third difference the resurrection of Jesus Christ can make in your life today. The apostles were arrested by the religious leaders and thrown into the public prison. That would be like the county jail. But, these human cells could not hold them. God freed them again and again with this message, "Go, stand in the temple and tell the people the whole message about this life."

The apostles had something to say with their lives. They were to tell others about Jesus Christ. So, obedient to their instructions, "they entered the temple at daybreak and went on with their teaching."

Through their lives — their words and their actions — the apostles told others about Jesus Christ. They were witnesses. Sometimes they were thrown in jail for this. Sometimes they were stoned for this. Sometimes they were beheaded for this. But, these things did not stop them. They had something to say. The resurrection of Jesus Christ compelled them to say it, whatever the costs to their personal comfort or safety. If Jesus is raised from the dead, there could be no more important news in the world to share!

We think the news is important. There are entire channels on television devoted to reporting the news. Radio carries news on the hour. When a story breaks, especially one of international proportions, it is common to interrupt other broadcasting to share the up-to-the-minute details. It is a rare person who will not talk about the latest happenings in the news and share opinions about them.

The greatest news flash the world has ever heard is this: "Why do you seek the living among the dead? He is not here, but has risen." Here is something worth talking about, sharing with family and friends and neighbors and strangers. Death is swallowed up in victory. God rules! Jesus is Lord!

How are you saying that with your life? How are your words and deeds shaped by that truth? How are others hearing that message of Christ's resurrection from your life? You have something to say with your life now! Jesus is risen! Say it loud and clear, so that when people see you or think of you or talk about you, they see Jesus, they think about Jesus, they talk about Jesus. You will come and go in their lives. Jesus will remain forever. Give them Jesus, *the* priceless treasure for all time and eternity.

Parents, teach your children how to pray to Jesus and walk with Jesus each day of their little lives. Sunday School teachers and Confirmation teachers, teach your students more about Jesus so they may grow closer to him. Husbands and wives, teach each other how to love out of the power of Jesus' love for you both. Workers, teach your bosses and co-workers and those who work under you that your work is an offering to the living God, as you do it well. Friends, teach each other that because Jesus is risen from the dead, he can bond you together through all differences and hardships.

Jesus said to his disciples, "You shall be my witnesses." In the words of the Nike commercial, *just do it!* You have something to say with your life. That something is the gospel of Jesus Christ.

You can have joy in your life. You can have meaning in your life. You can have something to say with your life. That is the power of the resurrection, which cannot wait until the end of time to make a difference in your life. It begins today, as you have faith. This is eternal life, present as well as future. Amen.

www.ingramcontent.com/pod-product-compliance
Lightning Source LLC
Chambersburg PA
CBHW071735040426
42446CB00012B/2365